Life through the eyes of a PK

ONE GOAL　　TWO VIEWS

AUVI CANADY & NIKKI CANADY-BOYD

Life through the eyes of a PK

ONE GOAL TWO VIEWS

AUVI CANADY & NIKKI CANADY-BOYD

T&J Publishers

A SMALL INDEPENDENT PUBLISHER WITH A BIG VOICE

Printed in the United States of America by
T&J Publishers (Atlanta, GA.)
www.TandJPublishers.com

© Copyright 2018 by Nikki Canady-Boyd & Auvi Canady

All rights reserved. This book or parts thereof may not be reproduced in any form, stored in a retrieval system, or transmitted in any form by any means-electronic, mechanical, photocopy, recording, or otherwise-without prior written permission of the author, except as provided by United States of America copyright law.

Cover Design by Timothy Flemming, Jr. (T&J Publishers)
Book Format/Layout by Timothy Flemming, Jr.

ISBN: 978-1-7324905-6-7

To contact author, go to:

Facebook: Nikki Canady-Boyd
Instagram: Pastor_Nikki
Twitter: PastorNikkiCB
Facebook: Auvi Canady-Jones

DEDICATIONS

This book is dedicated to every PK, no matter your age. From a pastor and a preacher's kid's perspective, we can identify with you. As a pastor, we understand that there are many hats you may have to wear in the course of a day. As a preacher's kid, we understand that you are just like any other kid with no spotlight!

Thank you to our family and friends who pushed us to finish this project together as we endeavored to bring to light one goal with two different views.

PASTOR NIKKI CANADY-BOYD'S THANKS

Thank you to my husband, Pastor Kimball Boyd. I appreciate your sacrifice and support, which you've given me during this time. Signed #OurSecondChance

I would like to thank Pastor Monica Haskell, my empowerment coach. Thank you for pushing me beyond my normal capabilities. Signed #PM Global Student.

Thank you to my professor, Nannette Floyd Patterson. Thank you for your effortless training as I became a Christian Life Coach.

Thank you Prophetess April Washington for your continual intercession for our ministry and our PK's. Your labor is not in vain, and your fruit shall remain.

To Apostle IV Hilliard and Pastor Bridget Hilliard, thank you for your continued faith teachings that have carried me through seasons of uncertainty in my life and ministry.

To every pastor, we hope to bring clarity to you to help during your building process in the ministry. To every PK, we pray that people will learn how to see life through your eyes.

Last, but not least, to Harvest Springs Ministries, thank you for riding the wave of ministry with us! #HSMYouRock

AUVI CANADY'S SPECIAL DEDICATION

To my late dad, Adrian Canady, daddy, I miss you so much! Words cannot express how much I wish I could talk to you once more. I dedicate my first book to you. I know you'd be proud of me. The things you prayed for, I'm finally doing. Your prayers were not in vain. Thank you daddy for being such a man of character and integrity. I will strive daily to make you proud. Your only girl, Auvi.

"You don't choose your family. They are God's gift to you, as you are to them."—Desmond Tutu

Table of Contents

INTRODUCTION	IT'S A FAMILY AFFAIR	11
CHAPTER 1	HELP!! MY CHILD IS RUINING OUR MINISTRY!	17
CHAPTER 2	I DIDN'T ASK FOR THE JOB, BUT I'LL TAKE IT	31
CHAPTER 3	IT'S COMPLICATED	47
CHAPTER 4	JUST A LITTLE RESPECT	61
CHAPTER 5	OVERCOMING STEREOTYPES	73
CHAPTER 6	LESSONS FROM MY PARENTS	89

PASTOR NIKKI'S AND AUVI'S COMMANDMENTS	99
PERSPECTIVES FROM TWO GENERATIONS	100

Introduction | Pastor Nikki

It's A Family Affair

For me, building a ministry has been an interesting journey. I've had to deal with loss, hardships, raising a family, as well as a church, with finding balance in the midst of a crazy, busy schedule, and more. I've had to deal with the challenges of not only being a pastor, but a female pastor of a growing congregation that my late husband and I started (perhaps, I'll save that for another book). I had to absorb the role of leadership after my late husband's sudden and unexpected death and acquire the knowledge to carry on with the ministry. I was not just a parent of four, but a *single*

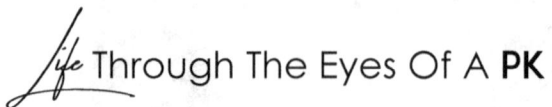

parent of four. It's been quite the experience. But it's been an experience made easier due to one thing, I didn't have to do it all alone. My greatest blessing has been being able to step into the leadership role with my family behind me, and more specifically, my oldest daughter, Auvi, working with me in ministry.

There are certain things that every ministry and business needs in order to become successful. It doesn't matter if you're running a church or a Fortune 500 company; without these things, you'll discover that success will fall out of your reach. One of the things you'll need is a spirit of excellence in whatever it is that you do. A few other things you'll need are to be accountable and responsible financially, brand and market yourself consistently, grow personally as a leader, and most importantly, realize that no one can succeed alone. We all need help. Our success in ministry and business depends on our relationships. You need to have people around you who are trustworthy, those who have your heart, and believe in your vision. In my case, my family has been my backbone. My daughter Auvi has been one of my biggest supporters and partners in the ministry. In fact, all of my children have been highly support-ive of me. Each of my kids had to be cool with sharing their mother with a congregation. They had to go through the dis-

> ...no one can succeed alone. We all need help. Our success in ministry and business depends on our relationships.

Introduction: It's A Family Affair

appointments with me when members hurt and attacked me. They had to help me bear a load they didn't sign up for. On top of it all, they made sure not to ruin my reputation as a pastor by embarrassing me in front of my congregation. They actually took a load off of my shoulders at the end of many long days, allowing me to recharge my battery. My kids made me laugh when I felt like crying, dance when I felt like slumping over. When I was down, they lifted my spirit and helped me to maintain a sense of balance in my life so that I didn't allow the ministry to ruin me personally.

As I stated earlier, I can speak to you from the perspective of a pastor, sharing with you the challenges that awaits one who starts a church from scratch and has to lead a congregation while dealing with the hurdles of sexism and personal loss. I can't speak to you about the experience of being a PK (preacher's kid) seeing that neither of my parents were preachers, but I realize that's a totally different experience. This role has its own set of challenges. From the outside, PKs certainly have their struggles. They have to put up with a lot, deal with a lot, face challenges the average kid doesn't have to face, deal with pressures that the average person doesn't have to deal with, and learn how to carry themselves in a manner that other kids don't have to conduct themselves. When it comes to understanding the mind and struggles of being a PK, that's where I have to step back and allow my daughter, Auvi to speak.

Regarding PKs, they tend to get a bad reputation. I'm sure you've heard it said before that PKs are some of the baddest kids on the planet. Many of them tend to stray completely away from the church and anything resembling the church.

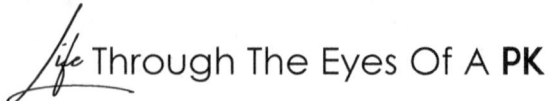 Through The Eyes Of A **PK**

Many PKs are quick to jump into destructive activities and behaviors. Some people may even refer to PKs as the spawn of Satan at times. There are reasons behind this type of behavior as Auvi will share. Auvi and I will reveal to you in the pages of this book is how to balance family and ministry or work, how to prioritize properly to ensure you don't become a public success and a private failure. We will further reveal how to establish a strong working relationship that allows you to work together in ministry and business so that you can accomplish everything that God has predestined for you to establish in this world and obtain every blessing God predestined for you to have on this earth.

It's possible to have family work alongside you in ministry—in fact, I'd go out on a limb to say that it's necessary to have your family by your side in your ministry or business. You need those who have your back to be beside you in that ministry. The family is God's first institution on the earth; it's what He established before there ever was a church. Marriage was God's first institution. He first made Adam and Eve and commanded them to "be fruitful and multiply" in the Garden of Eden. God made Adam and Eve a team and told them both to work the garden together. Both of them were told to have dominion over the earth. And today, as has been noted by many researchers, the family is the number one source of financial prosperity in this country. Many businesses start out as family businesses. In the old days, farmers relied on family members to help cultivate their lands, grow crops, and take care of the livestock. Some of them turned their family own farms into businesses like Hillshire Farms, Pillsbury, General Mills, and others. In fact, some of the biggest retail chains we

Introduction: It's A Family Affair

see today are family businesses: Walmart (started by the Walton family); Hobby Lobby (started in the Green family's garage); Volkswagen; Carnival Cruises, Enterprise, and more. No one knows you better than family. No one has your heart like family. With family, things can either go entirely right or entirely wrong. This all depends on your ability to communicate, get along, and establish healthy habits that allow you to remain on one accord.

Life Through The Eyes of a PK is a glimpse into the inner workings of a mother and daughter team. My daughter, Auvi, and I work together, and it's because of our ability to work together the way that we do that we've been able to accomplish so much more than I would have been able to accomplish on my own. She has her own mind, perspective, and way of doing things, and I have mine. We don't always see eye to eye, but that's the beauty of our relationship. By having different perspectives, we're able to recognize different problems and reach new demographics. She is from the younger generation and I'm more old school, but by bringing our different perspectives together we're able to be more multi-generational in our church. The elders need the energy of the youth and the youth need the wisdom of the elders. It's about recognizing the value in your differences rather than criticizing your differences. Through gaining a better understanding of one another, Auvi and I have learned how to build together in ministry, and that's what we're going to teach you how to do. I hope you're ready. Let's get started.

1 | Pastor Nikki

Help!! My Child Is Ruining Our Ministry!

I WILL NEVER FORGET THE DAY MY DAUGHTER AUVI CAME to me and told me that she was pregnant. *Not my baby!* I thought. It didn't matter that she was twenty years old; she was still my baby. *A parent will never fully stop seeing their child as their baby.* As you can imagine, word of her pregnancy spread throughout the church swiftly. "Hey, did you hear what happened? Auvi is pregnant." "Girl, I just heard the pastor's daughter is pregnant?" Chatter like this filled the air

Life Through The Eyes Of A PK

whenever members of the church got together. This became the main topic of discussion on the telephone during member gossip sessions. Auvi and I could feel the pressure whenever we walked into the church. Some people would get silent and stare at us. It was tough to deal with.

Everyone knew Auvi wasn't married. They knew she was young and single. They saw her grow up in the church listening to her father and mother preach and teach about the importance of waiting until marriage before becoming sexually active. She knew right from wrong. She has her own brain. But unlike myself when I was young and pregnant while unmarried, Auvi had the entire church to deal with. I didn't have to deal with that pressure. I didn't have an entire congregation looking down on me for my mistakes. I didn't grow up in church. I spent my time in the streets clubbing and trafficking drugs. My mother and I didn't have the best relationship, so I struggled with handling many of the transitions in my life. Auvi had much more pressure on her shoulders throughout this entire ordeal. She was under the weight of expectations that could have crushed her had she not had a strong support system behind her growing up. To be honest, I, too, was under immense pressure. As the First Lady of the church, I entertained the idea that I am responsible for setting the example for godly living in front of the congregants. I wrestled with the idea of preaching against the sin of fornication while my unmarried daughter wobbled through the sanctuary with a baby in her womb in full view of everyone. I could have thought to myself, "What an embarrassment! How could she have let us down? Doesn't she know that whenever she does something bad, the people look at me as her mother and won-

Chapter 1: Help!! My Child Is Ruining Our Ministry!

der if I'm a suitable leader? After all, if I can't straighten out my own kids and lead them into the straight and narrow path, how can I effectively lead others?

Both Auvi and I faced a lot of pressure. I was concerned about my image as First Lady and she was concerned about whether or not she had brought shame upon us before the church. She was already feeling beaten up inside for not taking all of the precautions to not get pregnant; and now, she was beating herself up even more with worry over how her actions might have affected our image. This was one of those pivotal moments where having the right perspective is crucial because having the wrong one can and will break you.

> It's easy to tell others to forgive and show love and acceptance to those who've messed up while forgetting to do the same for those who are in your own household.

You can't stop life from happening. You can't prevent mistakes from occurring. I have learned as an individual that you are not perfect and neither can you be. Every so often, these types of occurrences come to remind us of that. They help us to rediscover what it means to be human, to authentically live life, and they teach us how to apply the same principles to our lives that we teach others to apply to their own lives. It's easy to tell others to forgive and show love and acceptance to those who've messed up while forgetting to do the same for those who are in your own household. If your kids ever mess up, will you forgive them and show them love and forgiveness? If your kids were perfect, how would you understand what it's like to practice godlike behavior towards them?

I think that we, as parents, and especially as pastors, forget that our children aren't special and that they aren't different from other children. We forget that our children are just like every other child. They have shortcomings, they make mistakes, they experience failures, they get tempted, they make the wrong decisions at times, they sometimes find themselves being led astray from God's path for their lives, they grapple with questions about God and wrestle with their faith as Believers (if they are Believers in Christ), and they miss the mark just like the rest of us (the word "sin" literally means "to miss the mark"). We believe that our children are supposed to be perfect versions of ourselves so that we can impress the rest of the world by showcasing them as trophies. We think their mistakes are a reflection of our own failures as parents, and we'd like to think any successes they've achieved in life are directly attributed to our involvement in their lives and affairs as parents—we'd like to believe that. But the truth is our children are their own individuals. They think on their own and act independently of us. They must make up their own minds and make their own decisions in life, and ultimately, they must stand before God and give an account of the lives they've lived on their own. We, as parents, won't be allowed to intervene and advocate on their behalves when they stand before God in judgment.

We must disentangle this big ball of mental and emotional yarn. You are not responsible for another person's

Chapter 1: Help!! My Child Is Ruining Our Ministry!

actions. If a person was raised wrong, they still have the internal awareness of right and wrong according to Romans 2:14-15. Your effectiveness as a leader isn't determined by your ability to create perfect children; but rather, it is determined by your ability to pattern your life after Christ and love imperfect children into health and wholeness. That's what I learned. That's what I had to apply to my relationship with my baby girl.

> Take the pressure off of yourself as a pastor, First Lady, and a parent. Choose to be a Christian... rather than a dictator who puts excessive pressure on your kids to out-perform every other child.

Take the pressure off of yourself as a pastor, First Lady, and a parent. Choose to be a Christian (a follower of Christ and His example) rather than a dictator who puts excessive pressure on your kids to out-perform every other child. By putting this kind of pressure on your kids, you'll end up creating a bigger monster than you can handle by making them resent you and the church.

Avoiding Creating Monsters

I've talked to pastors whose number one concern is over the type of image their children are portraying and how that image is negatively affecting their ministry. These pastors are scared that their children are going to sink their ministries like that iceberg did the Titanic. They are afraid that their children's lack of academic achievements in school will make it appear as if they aren't parenting them properly; hence, their

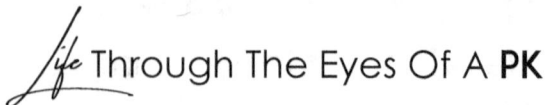

less than impressive academic performances. Some of these pastors even believe that the anointing that's on their lives is supposed to cause their children to become geniuses—they think their children's performances and actions are supposed to prove they're truly anointed and favored by God. The irony of this is the more they try to whip their kids into shape so that their kids will stop embarrassing them as church leaders, the more they create resentment in their kids and therefore cause them to act in an embarrassing manner.

Resentment creates monsters out of those we love. The word resentment means "bitter indignation at having been treated unfairly" (Webster's Dictionary). Our kids actually begin to feel as if we, as parents, are treating them unfairly when we prioritize our images over their need for love and acceptance. They begin to feel as if they're second-place in our lives next to the church when we're more concerned about how we look to the church than how we look to them.

> "Resentment creates monsters out of those we love."

I didn't want Auvi to feel like she was second-place in my life next to the church. Any correction that I brought to her, I had to be careful to do so with the right motivation. My motivation for correcting her couldn't be because I feared she was ruining my image and reputation around the church; instead, I had to communicate to her that I was genuinely concerned about her wellbeing. *'Auvi, don't drink because it will destroy your body'* as opposed to *'Auvi, don't drink because it will make me look bad in front of the members of the church.'*

Chapter 1: Help!! My Child Is Ruining Our Ministry!

When everything is about the church, your child will feel as if they are less important in your eyes, and that's what will prompt them to act out even more just to get your attention and prove to you that "THEY EXIST AND THEY MATTER!" This works the same way in marriage, friendships, and in other intimate relationships. Your children don't want to be pastored. Your spouse doesn't want to be pastored. Your parents don't want to be pastored. Your best friend from childhood also will have issues with you trying to pastor them. These people want to know that they are truly and genuinely important to you even beyond the church. They want to know that you appreciate and value them for who they are, flaws and all and that you're not trying to use them to make yourself look impressive in front of a church or organization.

I showed Auvi all of the love, respect, appreciation, and acceptance that I would have shown to anyone else while she was pregnant. I stood firm on what the Word of God says about sex outside of marriage, but I also demonstrated the compassion, gentleness, empathy, and love that Christ would have demonstrated to her and anyone else who messed up. Jesus didn't condemn people, He liberated them from guilt and shame and reconciled them to the Heavenly Father. In 1 Corinthians 13:4-8, God reveals to us what being a Christian really looks like:

> *4* Love is patient and kind. Love is not jealous or boastful or proud
> *5* or rude. It does not demand its own way. It is not irritable, and it keeps no record of being wronged.
> *6* It does not rejoice about injustice but rejoices

whenever the truth wins out.

7 Love never gives up, never loses faith, is always hopeful, and endures through every circumstance.

8 Prophecy and speaking in unknown languages and special knowledge will become useless. But love will last forever! (New Living Translation)

Your kids aren't moved by how well you can prophesy or speak in tongues. When they see you operating in spiritual gifts at church while neglecting them at home, they'll begin to question your faith and wonder how God can speak to you about everyone else's situation, but not speak to you about the situation in your own home. They'll even gain a tainted view of Christianity, believing that it doesn't produce authentic, genuine changes in people lives because they don't see it producing a change in their home and personal life. Love is what moves the hearts of others and it is what's going to win over the heart of your own family.

The one thing I'm determined to do is prioritize properly when it comes to my family and the ministry. My first ministry is my home. Before there was a church, God created the family. Before there were any church members, it was me and my first husband, Adrian, and our kids. God blessed me to remarry after the death of my first husband, and it is me and my husband's understanding that we are to be our first priority. Focusing on our family is number one. (I'll talk a little bit more about what this means in another chapter, but for now, it is important that family be your first priority.)

Some people place ministry at the top of their list of priorities and their families suffer for it. Their kids grow up

Chapter 1: Help!! My Child Is Ruining Our Ministry!

feeling neglected and pushed out. Their spouses feel as if they have to compete with the church or ministry for their attention and affection. Resentment builds in the children and they act out in rebellion towards the church whom they see as competition in the struggle to receive love from their parents. Resentment builds in spouses who also see the church or ministry as competition, and

> "I understood then as I do now that my first ministry is my home. Before there was a church, God created the family."

these spouses begin to act out in subtle ways just to express their dissatisfaction. Communication in the home begins to suffer also. The kids will start to turn away from the church and begin seeking guidance and acceptance elsewhere and the spouses will begin to look for attention elsewhere.

Sadly, the reason some people have wrongly placed ministry at the top of their priorities list is that they've been misled into believing that loving their families more than the church is the same as loving men more than God. That's not true. According to Ephesians 5:22-29, the Apostle Paul makes it clear that our love for God is demonstrated through the act of loving our families. Also, 1 Timothy 5:8 declares, "But those who won't care for their relatives, especially those in their own household, have denied the true faith. Such people are worse than unbelievers" (NLT). So, it is clear that by ignoring and neglecting one's family, they are actually dishonoring God. Jesus didn't tell us that if we love *the church* more than we love our families we would be worthy of Him in Matthew 10:37. He said if we put following people above following Him, then we would be unworthy of Him—and by "following people" that includes people in the church. Some people follow their church and its denomination more than they do God, which is a problem. So the emphasis is on simply doing what Jesus instructs us to do in Scripture, not professing our undying allegiance to an organization or institution. The church comes second to family. Christ and His Word comes first. Christ tells us in His Word to take care of our homes and families above all else. He even warns the husbands in 1 Peter chapter 3, that if they mistreat their wives their prayers will be hindered, and He tells wives in that same chapter that having a meek and gentle spirit towards their husbands is "precious in the sight of God" and that it demonstrates that we, as wives, actually trust God just as Sarah did. It's not God or family; it's God and family. Ignoring your family will actually lead to the destruction of your ministry.

Being that family is at the top of my list, I made it a point of becoming friends with my children and focusing on showing them as much love and acceptance as I possibly could even above that of my ministry. I can't stress how important becoming my children's friend is and how much it actually blessed my ministry.

Again, the household I was raised in wasn't a church-going one. I didn't have the best relationship with my mom. My parents divorced when I was very young, so I didn't have that picture-perfect family. But one thing I was determined to do was disallow what I didn't receive as a child growing up to hinder me from being the best mom I could be. Since my mom and I didn't truly become friends until I was in my adult years, I decided to break that cycle (that curse) and give my

Chapter 1: Help!! My Child Is Ruining Our Ministry!

children what I didn't get growing up. I decided that I was going to make it so that my kids could talk to me about anything—and I do mean anything—that was on their minds. Of course, that "anything" included sex. That was a big one. In fact, it was this open, honest, non-judgmental communication that enabled me to guide my daughter in the right direction after her pregnancy. Auvi knew that she could talk to me about anything, and she did. When she broke the news of the pregnancy to me, I didn't judge her for it. I began to give her some advice. Listening to the wrong voices, Auvi had come under the belief that the only way to make things right was to marry the young man she had sex with and had been impregnated by. She was even more concerned about what church people thought about her than I was, and I was the First Lady. I let her know that we will take care of the baby as a family and that she didn't need to make the mistake of marrying out of some misguided sense of obligation—that it didn't matter what anyone at that church thought about her, I accepted her and she was loved, and she didn't have to prove anything to anyone. This strengthened the bond between us even more.

> "I can't stress how important becoming my children's friend is and how much it actually blessed my ministry."

Becoming my children's friend challenged me as a parent in a major way. As parents, we tend to operate more in ego when it comes to our children. For example, if we do wrong by them, we don't feel it is necessary for us to apologize to them. I can't explain why this is the case for so many parents. Maybe some parents think that apologizing to their children is beneath them, which is also a way of communicating that their children's feelings are beneath them. Perhaps some parents feel as if they're entitled to ignore their children's feelings on the account of the fact that they have provided for them throughout the years, but then again, it is abusive to mistreat someone simply because you know they need and depend on you. One of the thoughts that often crossed my mind is, "If I, as a mother, am willing to treat strangers better than I treat my own children, then I'm not that good of a person in general." I should at least treat my friends better than I do my enemies and my family better than I do anyone else. Why? It's because at the end of the day, once all else is gone and everyone has parted and gone their separate ways, all we'll have left is family. Church members come and go, but your family will always be there.

When establishing a friendship with your children, it's important that you maintain open communication about everything that is on your hearts and minds, especially the things that offend you. Start with the small things. Talk about the small things you like and dislike that each of you does. Respect the fact that your children may dislike certain things that you do; they do, after all, have minds of their own. Allow one another to talk without getting angry or offended. Listen objectively to understand one another and gain a better understanding of one another.

I can recall once when Auvi grew frustrated and flustered with me. She had a very important occasion for celebra-

Chapter 1: Help!! My Child Is Ruining Our Ministry!

tion in her life and I explained to her that I wasn't going to be able to attend. She grew upset and expressed to me her feelings. She explained to me that she had been extremely busy planning so many celebrations for me—a pastor's celebration as well as my birthday celebration—and didn't think it was fair that I was bailing out of something that was a big deal to her just to accommodate a few members of the church and pastor friends. When I thought about it, I did realize that I was pushing her off for others rather than showing her appreciation. I could have gotten egotistical and went with the "I'm the parent, and you're the child" line, but that would have been unfair. I had to be willing to allow her to share her heart and express what bothered her, and then I had to push aside my ego and place myself in her shoes to understand where she was coming from. Now, there are times when I do have to remind my kids that I'm their parent, but I've trained them to know that they can be open and honest with me regarding what they're thinking and feeling and that I will also be open with them about the things in my heart and on my mind.

  Whenever I was wrong or insensitive to my children's needs, I apologized to them. I didn't become egotistical and make them feel like their feelings are unimportant to me. I let them know that their voices, opinions, and feelings are of equal, if not more, value as those I pastor. I refused to treat church members with more respect than I treated my own children. This type of attitude made all of the difference, but I will allow my daughter, Auvi to explain in the next chapter.

Life Through The Eyes Of A **PK**

Key Points

- As a parent and leader, quit expecting perfection out of your kids and yourself.
- See the mistakes of your children and of others as an opportunity for you to practice Christian compassion and love - after all, you'll need someone to be loving and compassionate towards you one day, too.
- Don't be so busy building your ministry or organization that you neglect to spend time building a relationship with your children.
- Learn to become your children's friend through open and honest communication, compassionate listening, mutual respect; by making them feel accepted, valued, and appreciated; and by balancing the time you devote to your home-life and your ministry or organization.
- Be humble and apologize to your children when you've wronged them as a parent.
- Obey God regardless of how anyone, including family, may feel about it.

2 | Auvi

I Didn't Ask For The Job, But I'll Take It!

PREACHERS' KIDS (PKs) ARE BORN INTO THIS WORLD wearing a crown of responsibility they didn't ask for. By virtue of the fact that their parents are leaders in the church, the responsibility of being role models for those within the church also falls into their laps. This is what most, if not all, PKs dislike about being PKs. They don't want to be forced into a role they didn't ask for. They don't want to have

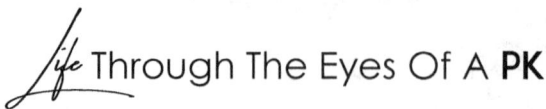# Through The Eyes Of A PK

people hold them to a higher standard than everyone else and then criticize them when they can't live up to that standard.

When a person chooses to become a pastor, they have already educated themselves on the standards and rules that apply to that position; and furthermore, they have already made up their minds that they want the role and responsibility that comes along with it. But in the case of a PK, they didn't choose this responsibility; they weren't educated into all of the responsibilities that come along with it. PKs have to learn church etiquette real fast and they have to embrace something they don't want while trying to live their own lives in the process. So, as you can imagine, there are a lot of internal battles taking place within them. They have to wrestle with living up to standards they believe are unfair, upholding standards their peers aren't being held to, put up with living in someone else's shadow while trying to gain respect as individuals, and most importantly, they have to live with the awareness that their every action can either build their parents' reputation in the ministry or tear it down. That's a lot of pressure placed on someone that was neither willing nor prepared mentally to deal with.

I, along with my younger siblings, understand that my mom had a job to do. She couldn't be around us all of the time and devote her every waking moment only to us—she had a church filled with people she also had to attend to. When your parents are leaders of a church, you have to accept the fact that you have to share them with others. Your parents will have to focus on you and other people's kids. That's the nature of the business. The definition of the word pastor is "shepherd." So, a pastor is someone who has to shepherd people as if they're

Chapter 2: I Didn't Ask For The Job, But I'll Take It

a flock of sheep, and that means constantly attending to them, watching out for them, protecting them from predators like wolves, keeping them fed, and helping them when they can't help themselves. Technically, a sheep is one of the dumbest animals on the planet, so a shepherd has to do almost everything for them. That's a lot of work and it requires a lot of dedication and commitment. It is one of the most time-consuming jobs there is. You really don't get a break. Even when you're on vacation you still have to run things from a distance. A church is just like a business; its structure is practically the same. Pastors have the same responsibilities as CEOs with the added bonus that they must deal with the whole man (spirit, soul, and body) and not just the physical man.

One of the main areas I assist my mom is in the business side of the church. I handle the finances; this includes dealing with outside vendors and contractors, staff, paying bills, making sure that the facilities remain up to code, etc. I do the administrative work. This is a business, a serious one. I see the load my mom has to deal with just running the business side of the church, let alone the ministry side (preparing sermons, visiting sick members, praying and interceding for members, attending trainings, etc.). So she has her hands full.

My siblings and I are aware of the fact that our mom wears many hats. She may be our mom, but she's also their pastor. She is also a wife. She has to be accountable to multiple people, not just us. That being the case, we realize that our actions can jeopardize everything she's worked hard to build. We can make her look good or bad. We can tear up her church or help to build it. If the church prospers, we prosper as a family. If the ministry goes down, our family would be negatively effected. We recognize the interconnectedness of the church/ministry and our home-life. We realize the power we have. As the old saying goes: *With great power comes great responsibility*.

Whenever mom would preach about family issues, undoubtedly, all eyes would glance over at me and my siblings. People would look to see our expressions at certain points during the message. People would read our expressions and behaviors just as intensely as they would listen to her words from the pulpit. Whether we liked it or not, we represented her in the church. To be honest, whether or not you like it, as Christians, we all represent God in and outside of the church walls.

> **To be honest, whether or not you like it, as Christians, we all represent God in and outside of the church walls.**

The Bible tells us as Christians in Romans 14:12 that "each of us will give a personal account to God" for our actions on this earth, but it also tells us in the next verse to "live in such a way that you will not cause another believer to stumble and fall" (vs. 13). So, although we are capable of living our lives any way that we choose to, we still have an obligation to live in a way that prevents other people from being misled. We shouldn't do things in front of others that will cause them to question our salvation. In other words, we still have to be accountable to others in the way that we live, we still represent God everywhere that we go. I may feel as if I

Chapter 2: I Didn't Ask For The Job, But I'll Take It

shouldn't have to answer to anyone for my actions as an individual adult, but I do and will. When I stand before God, I'll have to answer for every deed and even every word I spoke (Matthew 12:36) while on this earth. The same is to be said for all of us.

Being a PK, the reality that you represent another person is impressed upon you at an early age. Everything you do as a PK is seen as a reflection of your parent's actions. Whenever I would do wrong, people would automatically look at my mom and ask themselves, "What is Pastor Nikki teaching those children?" If I listened to some crazy music that was filled with profanity, sexual perversion, and other sinful messages, people would automatically look at my mom and ask, "Does Pastor Nikki allow her kids to listen to that type of music? Does she (Pastor Nikki) listen to that stuff, too?" That's the way people think. It's rare that people will think to themselves first, *'Well, Auvi is doing this or that because that's what she wants to do. This has nothing to do with Pastor Nikki.'* There's increased pressure on both the Pastor and the PK placed on them by the church. The tendency of PKs to rebel is because of this. Of course, we, PKs, didn't ask for this kind of pressure, we were born into it. We typically abhor this type of pressure. I have one Bible verse that always helps me to keep things in proper perspective so that I won't become bitter over the pressure others place on me to live a certain way. It's found in 1 Corinthians 6:19-20, which says,

> "Don't you realize that your body is the temple of the Holy Spirit, who lives in you and was given to you by God? You do not belong to yourself, for

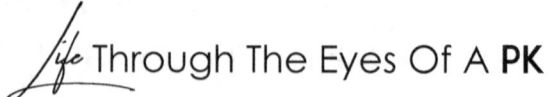 Through The Eyes Of A PK

God bought you with a high price. So you must honor God with your body." (NLT)

I'm reminded that my life is not my own, and that my body is God's property. I don't belong to men, to my parents, to the people at the church; I am the exclusive property of God. This lets me know that I don't have to live my life under the pressure from others, and that I don't have to be what others want me to be and live up to their expectations. That freed me; this also reminds me that everyday of my life there is one whose expectations I do have to live up to: God's. He's judge, jury, and executioner. He's also my Lord and Savior. My actions will be examined and judged by Him, not the people in the church.

Obeying God might even place me at odds with the wishes of the people inside and outside of the church, but I'm okay with that because I don't belong to anyone else besides the God who made me. I'm okay with being accountable to God and striving to live up to His expectations for my life. Only God is worthy of that type of devotion from me. Only He possesses the right to call me His property, His slave. He loves me unlike any other, and He's wiser than all others. I will gladly follow His advice, instructions, and guidance. Man? Not so, because people aren't worthy of God's glory and His praises.

I discovered that I am to be accountable to God above even my own parents. That's one of the biggest lessons my mom taught me and my siblings. She let us know early on that it doesn't matter what she or anyone else think about us, as long as we know what God thinks about us, that's all that

Chapter 2: I Didn't Ask For The Job, But I'll Take It

matters. She didn't train us to perform for the church; instead, she trained us to keep God on the forefront of our minds always and think about how our actions were affecting Him. This took a lot of the pressure off of our shoulders as PKs and let us feel the freedom to breathe around others. But being accountable to God also set us up to regulate our actions when around others. For as I mentioned earlier, God doesn't want us as His children to cause others to stumble in their faith through our bad examples. So, with this level of accountability hanging over my head, I became conscious of my actions and how they affected others even more than I would have had I been taught that my actions solely represent my mom and the church. Knowing who I'm really accountable to in life did a lot to set me straight, and it continues to be the guiding light in my life.

No, I'm not perfect. Who is? *You're certainly not.* Nor is anyone you or I know. But knowing God's Word gives me direction in life; it teaches me the right way to live. When I do mess up, having a relationship with the Holy Spirit for myself allows me to feel both the conviction and the love that I need to come out of that sin and repent and keep moving forward with my life. I choose to do the right thing out of love for God, not out of fear of being judged by others.

Living to please others will lead to resentment and bitterness, but living to please God will lead to peace, joy, and happiness. Why is this the case? Because God is love. Everything God does for us, He does out of love. Everything God gives to us, He gives out of love. Every instruction God gives us, He gives for our protection. Every plan He has for our lives is centered around His desire to bless and prosper us as

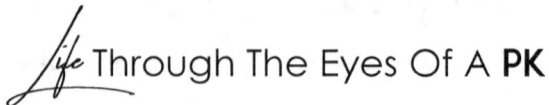 Through The Eyes Of A **PK**

declared in Jeremiah 29:11. Who wouldn't want to serve a God like that? Who wouldn't want to live for a God like that?

Love makes the difference.

I've encountered people who wanted to control me just to boost and stroke their own egos. I've encountered people who wanted to hold me to expectations they themselves can't even live up to. I've encountered people who wanted to make me what they wanted me to be and even live their lives vicariously through me. I've even encountered people who've tried to win me over so that they can turn me against my own mom. So believe me when I say that love is what makes the difference. People have all kinds of motives for trying to control you, but God only has one pure motive: He wants to pour out His love on you and give you the best that He has to offer. To top of this, He's our creator. That makes Him the only one worthy of your total devotion.

Respecting Mom

Love commands respect and devotion from others. When someone genuinely loves and cares about you, you feel more inclined to honor them. Some PKs unfortunately grow up in environments where they're not shown much love and respect at home, but then they're expected to pretend as if their family is so loving and supportive of one another while out in the public eyes. This is hypocrisy. When the love and respect isn't there in the home, don't expect that PK to *perform* in front of the people just to make you look like some great one. That's not going to happen. Even PKs who love God will expose the falsehood in your facade while out in public.

The truth is, you can't fake true happiness and fulfill-

Chapter 2: I Didn't Ask For The Job, But I'll Take It

ment. When the home-life isn't where it should be, the evidence of this disconnect in the home will surface in the behaviors of those involved. You can try to smile all you want, but when home is jacked-up people will begin to easily sense that you're just pretending to be happy.

There are Christian families where the members don't even talk, they don't even carry on conversations about the things that trouble them; they don't even embrace, hug, or show any type of affection. In some of these families, the kids are going crazy while dealing with things like sexuality and peer pressure and the parents' only concern is that they act like they're little angels when out in the public—they don't even discuss these things at home. In some homes, when these topics do come up, the parents respond with scorn and rebuke, saying stuff like, "The only thing you need to be thinking about is your education! Those books are your boyfriend, your girlfriend for the time being. I don't want to hear anything else about this." I honestly feel sorry for those families.

> "Living to please others will lead to resentment and bitterness, but living to please God will lead to peace, joy, and happiness."

One of the reasons I honor my mother not just at home, but around the ministry the way that I do is because she took the time to build a genuine relationship with me. This relationship is one that's built on love and a mutual respect. She could have shut me down each time I came to her about a boy. She could have avoided subjects such as boys and sex altogether. But, oh, not this mom. This mom was like an open book. No subject was off the table in our house. We heard it from her before we heard it from the streets and that made a huge difference in our lives growing up. Mom talked to me at an early age about the things my body was getting ready to go through (puberty). She explained the ins and outs to me about boys, sex, and other things before anyone else could. She created a non-judgment zone where my brothers and I felt comfortable talking to her about anything that was on our minds. But more important than that, she was totally transparent with us. She didn't pretend as if she grew up in a perfect home. In fact, she revealed just the opposite. She talked about her experiences with boys, with sex, with drugs and drug dealing, with being molested, with getting in fights, being involved with gangsters and being involved with gang activity. She revealed the things she wrestled with growing up, the questions she had about God and faith, the doubts and fears she had, her struggles with identity, with accepting her calling (thank God she didn't make it seem like she had always desired to be in the ministry), the struggles she faced in the ministry, etc. She respected our opinions and even asked for them, which made us feel as if we have a voice in her world. Our mother became our friend.

Because of the love, respect, and friendship that my mother and I possessed growing up, I gladly, even happily, made whatever changes necessary to protect her image and reputation around the church. To put it bluntly, I valued the ministry because it was so very important to her. Whatever was important to her was important to me. The thing I val-

Chapter 2: I Didn't Ask For The Job, But I'll Take It

ued the most was our relationship, and this meant valuing the things that matter to her the most.

When we show love and build friendships with others, their concerns become our concerns. We might not like and agree with everything they say and do, but if something is important to them, it is important to us also because it is important to them.

Contrary to what some people may believe, when you have a real friendship with someone, that friendship doesn't diminish the respect you have for them. Some people fear that by getting to close to others or allowing others to get too close to them, others will begin to lose respect for them. The truth is, every friendship is built on an understanding of roles and boundaries. A real friend won't try to use you for their personal gain; instead, they'll respect your boundaries, principles, values, cares and concerns. When respect for these boundaries and values is lost, that's when the friendship begins to crumble and fall apart. The thing you have to ask yourself is "Do I have a friend or a leach in my life?" A friend respects you and comes to enhance your life, whereas a leach comes to manipulate you and take away from your life. Some of us are simply mistaking leaches for friends.

> "...every friendship is built on an understanding of roles and boundaries. A real friend won't try to use you for their personal gain; instead, they'll respect your boundaries, principles, values, cares and concerns."

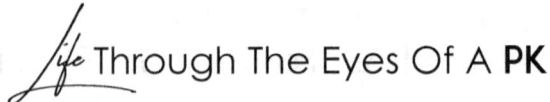 Through The Eyes Of A **PK**

God wants to establish a friendship with us as He explains in John 15:14. There, Jesus said, "You are My friends, if you do whatsoever I Command you" (KJV). Friends don't force each other to do anything. Friends do things for one another out of the love and respect they share for one another. God doesn't try to force us to obey Him. What God does is love us into His presence. He establishes a relationship with us based on love and respect. Why? Because He knows that if we love Him, we'll be more than glad to obey His commandments and honor Him (1 John 5:3). If we love God, we'll love what He loves and hate what He hates. Also, we'll value the things of God because they matter to Him. A church building doesn't really mean anything to me, but because it is the house of God, it is a place that matters to God. I respect it as more than just a building. I respect it as God's house. Likewise, you can tell who truly has a relationship with God: they'll respect the things that are important to God. Those who don't truly have a relationship with God won't value the things of God because they don't have that level of intimacy with Him to know and care about the things that are important to His heart.

Hold Up! This Is My Facebook Page!

I can recall once when I would hang out with a few of my friends, we would go to the clubs. During this time, I would drink you under the table. While partying and getting drunk, I would take selfies with my friends and post them on my Facebook page. Well, it didn't take long for the accusations and criticism to come pouring in. Members of my parents' church would see my pictures all over Facebook and then re-

Chapter 2: I Didn't Ask For The Job, But I'll Take It

port them back to my mom. They would talk and say all kind of mean and nasty things about my clubbing and drinking. Of course, my first mind was to tell them to stop trolling my page when my mom began confronting me about the matter. In my mind, mom was acting like the Facebook Police. She kept asking me to take certain pictures down. My first thought was, *'No. I need to know who these 'friends' of yours are that keep spying on my page so I can unfriend or block them from my page! This is my page!'* But then, the thing that began to melt my heart was the fact that what I was doing was hurting my mom's heart. I stopped thinking about the people and I started thinking about my mom's reputation, which I didn't want to tarnish. At that moment, I decided that whenever I did go out with my friends to the club, I wouldn't take pictures with them and post them on my social media pages. I didn't want my mom to face the embarrassment and deal with the harassment any further. After that, if anyone reported to my mom that they saw me getting drunk in the club, it was because they were in the club with me.

 Because of my love for my mom, I made it a point of mine to avoid doing things that would cause her public embarrassment and shame. If I didn't have this love in my heart for her—but instead carried resentment in my heart towards her—I probably would have taken a different attitude and become even more hard-hearted when faced with situations like the one I just mentioned.

 The word *honor* means "to give weight to." When you love someone, you want to honor them, which means you consider the things that are important to them to be high up on your list of values and priorities. If you love your hus-

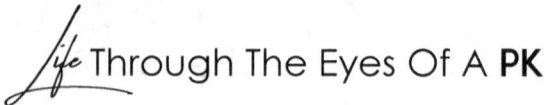

band, then the things that are important to him will also be important to you. You may not like football, but because he loves football you'll at least try to show an interest in it. Why? Because you want him to know that you love and appreciate everything about him, including his interests and hobbies and vice-versa.

It's because of my love for God and my mom that I serve in the ministry the way that I do. This love is what keeps me grounded when I want to snap on disrespectful people and when I want to walk away from it all. It is this love that causes me to consider my actions and how they affect God and my mom. Without love being the foundation for all of the things I do around the ministry, I wouldn't be doing them—I would probably be a bitter, angry, and defensive young woman with a chip on her shoulder and a point to prove to others. I'd be more fixated on my haters than I am on God, my bright future, my glorious destiny, and my loving family. That's what makes the difference in my life. That's what makes the difference in the life of every PK.

Chapter 2: I Didn't Ask For The Job, But I'll Take It

- Remember that as a preacher's kid (PK), your parent(s) have a great responsibility on their hands to lead others. Do as much as you can to help them fulfill the divine calling on their lives rather than try to hinder them.
- As a PK, your actions and lifestyle choices will affect your parents' ministry.
- As a PK, you are born with influence. You are also in a leadership position whether you know it or not. Use your influence as a leader to focus others' attention on God.
- Focus on being accountable to God in all that you do, not on pleasing people. Remember: you are accountable to God as an individual. So always think about how your actions affect God, not people.
- Focus on loving God and drawing close to Him for yourself.

3 | Pastor Nikki

It's Complicated

I ENJOY HAVING MY DAUGHTER WORK ALONGSIDE ME IN THE ministry. I'll admit that there are times when I have to remind my daughter that I'm still the mom, and then there are times when I have to remind her that I'm a pastor. Yeah, it can get complicated. It's something you have to get used to. Once those boundaries have been established, however, the rest is smooth sailing.

One of the biggest challenges many pastors have is setting boundaries and sticking to them. Boundaries are important because they teach people how to treat you. When you're in the ministry, it's very important that you set boundaries so that people will know how to treat you, address you

properly, respect the title and position you hold, and respect the anointing that's on your life. You do a disservice to both yourself and those you lead when you fail to establish rules and guidelines for interactions.

Many times ministry leaders will get upset over disrespectful behavior from their members. The reality is if you don't teach people how to address you, you can't get angry with them for wrongly addressing you and overstepping their boundaries—you never laid down boundaries.

Boundaries aren't enemies of success. Jesus laid down boundaries among His disciples. He allowed certain disciples to accompany Him in certain places. He didn't let all of them accompany Him when it was time for Him to perform certain miracles. He'd often take Peter, James, and John with Him when performing certain tasks. Why? It's because these three held a stronger level of respect for His ministry. Jesus loved each of His disciples, but He only granted access to certain individuals to enjoy a higher level of intimacy with Him. In that same way, as leaders, we pick and choose who gets to enjoy higher levels of closeness with us based off of their level of respect for us and their level of maturity. Everyone who smiles at you isn't fit to be your armor-bearer. Everyone who acts kind isn't prepared to deal with certain aspects of you. Some people need to only see you as Pastor; they don't need to come any closer because they don't know how to handle you outside of the church setting. I'll go out with certain people to the movies and out to eat, but

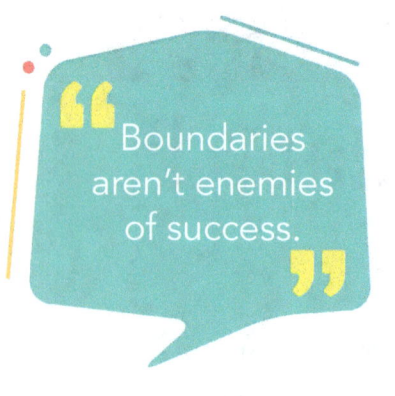

"Boundaries aren't enemies of success."

Chapter 3: It's Complicated

I won't do those things with most people. Why? Because it's important to maintain a level of respect among your followers.

In Romans chapter 14, the Apostle Paul addressed the dynamics of respect in relationships. He used the example of new believers who were opposed to eating meats that had been dedicated to idol gods. In Romans 14:21-22, the Apostle Paul explains that if one believer sees nothing wrong with eating meats offered to idols because they know whom they worship then they shouldn't be so inconsiderate of the new believer who does see something wrong with eating those meats. He says the more seasoned believer must not cause the newer believer to stumble by doing something in front of them that would cause them to stumble in their faith. The key is to avoid doing certain things in front of individuals that aren't mature enough to handle seeing you do those things.

Let me use another example to illustrate this. Let's say that, as a pastor, I am at a restaurant with a group of members from my church and there are glasses of wine on the table in front of us. As a pastor, I am familiar with the biblical teaching on drinking wine. I know that the Apostle Paul prescribed red wine to his son in the ministry, Timothy, to help with an upset stomach. I know that the Jews used wine in all of their celebrations—it was a cultural symbol of rejoicing. I also know all of the warnings in Scripture against being drunk with wine. Still, despite knowing all of this, as the pastor, it is my responsibility to be conscious of whom I'm sitting at the table with. I have to be aware of the fact that these same people I'm sitting with have to hear me preach and teach after that. So, I have to make sure not to make it difficult for them to respect me as a minister; therefore, although I could drink the wine, I choose not to. Also, because of the deliverance that took place in my life as it relates to drinking and smoking, I just choose not to open those doors in my life. When they begin to talk about certain things, I have to be cautious about what words I allow to proceed out of my mouth. Certain conversations I can't engage in with members. Certain places I can't go with members. Now, if I'm with my husband, that's a different story. Although I don't drink, I do enjoy dancing with my husband to the oldies. I can let loose and relax with him. If I'm with a group of my preacher friends who understand what it means to be a pastor and a normal human, certain conversations I can and will have that I won't have with others. This may sound depressing and restricting, but it's a part of the territory of being a leader. Jesus said we must count the cost before accepting a position and taking on a role. Jesus told us "to whom much is given much is required" in Luke 12:48.

> ...being in a leadership role simply means you have more responsibility and you have to tread more carefully than the average person.

So being in a leadership role simply means you have more responsibility and you have to tread more carefully than the average person. As a leader, your mistakes are magnified, your actions are more closely scrutinized, and your words are more closely examined. If an average person were to make a racist tweet, it would not make the news; but if the President of the United States were to send out a racist tweet, it would be covered by CNN, Fox News, MSNBC, BBC, and

Chapter 3: It's Complicated

every other major news source and media outlet. When you want the spotlight, you have to be ready for the responsibility that comes with it. You don't get to pick and choose.

LAYING DOWN THE LAW

Before you try to set boundaries with others, set boundaries with yourself first. Make sure that you discipline your life. Have strong ethics, a good code of conduct, and an understanding of who you are first. How can others respect you if you don't respect yourself? How can others properly address you if you don't understand your role, title, and position, and have a sense of identity?

One of the things that I make sure to do is remind myself of who I am on a constant basis, especially when it comes to different settings and dealing with certain people. I have to remind myself at times that I'm still mom so that I won't allow the pastoral role to interrupt my obligations as a parent. I have to remind myself when at home that I'm a wife to my husband so that I won't address him wrongly and bring tension into my marriage. I can be a pastor at the church and a wife and mother at home. I know when to take off the mom hat and put on the pastor hat when facing certain situations. I have learned that each role carries its own set of responsibilities and how to be what is necessary for each situation. <u>At the root of it all, I know that I am first and foremost a child of God; and furthermore, I realize that in every situation I have to turn to and lean on the guidance of the Holy Spirit to know what to be and what to do in every situation.</u> The Holy Spirit will give me that wisdom in different situations to know when I need to take off a certain hat and put on another. That's the key to it all. Pray about every situation and ask God to guide you on how to successfully handle it.

Knowing what the role of a pastor entails, I am better equipped to instruct the members of my church on how to address me. I know how to instill a true sense of respect in them for my title and position. As I've explained to them, as pastor my responsibility is to God first. I have to make sure I'm following God, not them. I let them know that I respect and value their opinions, but I have to make sure I'm walking in alignment with God's will for the ministry. Some people may get upset about that, but they know early on that they can't rule and control me. It doesn't matter how much they give and how much they support me. If God tells me to do something they don't agree with then they'll have to either go along with it or leave because God's word is final.

Furthermore, I teach others to respect the office that I hold. In the military, you're taught to honor and acknowledge ranks, and the same goes for the ministry. The pastor is the leader - they're God's leader. God put them in position, not the people. So, to attack that leader is to question God's decision and judgment. You may not like the person God decides to use in the ministry, but that's something you'll have to take up with Him.

In 1 Samuel chapter 26, David was on the run from King Saul who had become demon possessed and demented. King Saul set out to kill David. In one particular instance, David was hiding in a cave with one of his comrades, Abishai, when King Saul entered in and laid down to get some rest. King Saul was completely unaware of the fact that David was hiding in the very cave he was resting in. King Saul then fell

Chapter 3: It's Complicated

asleep. David had the perfect opportunity to kill the man who had been hunting him, but he instead uttered these words to his comrade who was encouraging him to kill the king:

> "And David said to Abishai, Destroy him not: for who can stretch forth his hand against the LORD'S anointed, and be guiltless? David said furthermore, As the LORD liveth, the LORD shall smite him; or his day shall come to die; or he shall descend into battle, and perish. The LORD forbid that I should stretch forth mine hand against the LORD'S anointed: but, I pray thee, take thou now the spear that is at his bolster, and the cruse of water, and let us go."

This is a prime example of respecting the title and position that God has placed on a person's life. King Saul was a murderous lunatic trying to kill David and David still refused to place a hand on him and do him harm. David understood that, although King Saul was wrong, it was up to God to remove him from power. David didn't stay there and allow himself to be killed—he did have common sense. David was respectful enough of the title and the anointing that was on King Saul's life to not harm him. He continued to pray for King Saul. He continued to trust in God rather than try to play God.

  These are the type of messages that have to be taught to congregants. It's important that people understand that it is God's job to appoint and remove a pastor. God knows how to deal with His vessels. Respecting that title and position is about respecting God, not the person who holds it. This establishes the most important boundary in ministry: respecting the anointing and the position rather than the personality.

Now, when it comes to the other hats I wear (wife, mother, etc.), the same rules apply. I explained to my kids what the Bible says about parent/child relationships. In Exodus 20:12, the Bible tells children to honor their parents so that their days may be long upon the earth. Dishonoring our parents will lead to an early grave. Dishonoring our parents will cause God to lift His hand off of our lives. As I've explained to them, by honoring me and their father, they are honoring God and setting up their futures for great success. Ultimately, they're still accountable to God—they're accountable to God for the way they treat my husband and me as their parents. They have to answer to God at the end, not us if they disrespect us. They also have to do as David did and pray for us if we're in the wrong. We train them to do what God instructs us to do in His Word regardless of who tells them otherwise—Jesus did say in Matthew chapter 10 that if we love our parents, children, and love-ones more than Him then we're not worthy of Him, which means we're not to obey others (including our parents) over God. As long as we're not instructing them to do that which is blatantly wrong, God instructs them to honor us as their parents. As parents, we have a responsibility to guide our children, protect them, train them up in the way that they should go, and instill in them the right values. Although I'm their friend, I'm still their mom, and they know that. They can sense when I'm putting on the mom hat and speaking from a position of authority.

To balance everything out, my first responsibility towards my children is to be their mother; my next responsibil-

Chapter 3: It's Complicated

ity is to be their friend. If I ever need to figure out which hat I need to wear when faced with a situation, I know to instinctively step into the role of "mother" first and make sure I've ruled out any potential dangers that may be waiting to entrap them. If I know there's danger at a certain party or there's danger in hanging out with a certain individual or they're about to stray into drugs and other dangerous things, I'm going to address them first as mom and let them know that I don't approve of what they're doing or who they're hanging out with and I'm going to explain to them the dangers that are awaiting them. When the threat has been addressed and cleared, that's when I can safely slip into friend mode and address them from that angle. As their mom, I'm here to protect them. As their friend, I'm here to connect with them.

When my first husband died, I lived single for a short time until Kimball and I decided to date. I already knew him. He was our friend and an elder in our church. After getting remarried, Kimball and I brought our kids together and created a blended family. Sometimes this can get a little tricky. Step-children don't always feel inclined to respect their step-parents. I gave my children the option to call my new husband Mr. Kimball, dad, or whatever they felt he was to them. I didn't want him referred to as step-dad. He stepped in and took on the responsibility of being a father, a strong masculine figure in the lives of my children, especially my sons. They needed that. But my kids understood early on that by respecting him they were respecting me, and vice-versa. They know that Kimball is my second chance and he's also their new father (or bonus dad as Auvi calls him). My husband and I approach our kids as a unified team and let them

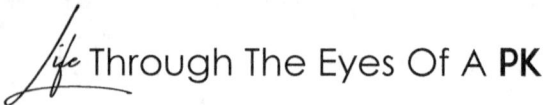 Through The Eyes Of A **PK**

know that there are no cracks in our armor; so when they disrespect one of us, they are going to hear it from both of us. If you have a blended family, this may take some work and your kids may even put your union to the test, but as long as you and your chosen mate remain consistent and on the same page the kids will begin to get the message. The key, however, is that the two of you must settle your differences beforehand, understand one another's expectations before you meet with the children, come to a conclusion together, and then present the rules for the household together. As a wife and mother, I allow Kimball to take the lead in setting the rules while I back him. It's important that my kids see me honoring and respecting my husband as the head of the household so that they can establish a sense of respect for him. Of course, the two of us have to be in agreement before we do anything, but I let the instructions flow from the head to instill this respect in my kids. When families operate as God intends for them to operate, His blessings will fall on that household.

Kimball and I operate in ministry together. We both possess the understanding as far as our roles go around the ministry. Being that our church was started by my late husband, Adrian, and me, I am still in the role as the co-founder and senior pastor of the church. God blessed me with a husband that loves and respects the position God has placed me in and he backs and supports me 100%. This is why the Bible tells us as Christians to avoid being "unequally yoked" with people who aren't going in the same direction as us in life. We add trouble to our lives when we hook up with people who are led by their flesh rather than by God's Spirit. Kimball didn't come into my life with a huge ego, acting as if I was

Chapter 3: It's Complicated

beneath him and trying to take over. He actually encouraged me to continue to be the person God called me to be and do what God called me to do, and this made me want to honor and love him even more. We are on one accord in ministry. I am still the senior pastor, but the members show him the same level of respect in the church. However, when I get home, I'm no longer Pastor Nikki; I'm Kimball's wife. I don't dictate to my husband at home. I may make the final decisions regarding the ministry, but I submit to my husband at home. This is a challenge for most women, but when women have a hard time operating in that feminine energy at home they tend to drive their husbands away. You can be the boss at the job, but your husband isn't your employee at home; he's your covering, your head.

Probably the most difficult thing for first families in ministry to do is work together because of the many roles and boundaries that apply to the different situations they encounter. For example, at church, my kids know me as Pastor. Outside of the church, my kids know me as their mom. At times, my kids have to remember that I'm their mom while inside of the church and know that if they embarrass "Pastor" in the church they'll have to face "mom" at home. It can get complicated. I know. You must develop a rhythm if you're going to do this

> You can be the boss at the job, but your husband isn't your employee at home; he's your covering, your head.

57

successfully. At times, I've had to deal with Auvi as Pastor and then console her as her mom. I had to get used to being so many people at one time, and I had to do this without losing my sense of self. These may be roles I take on, but I am not a role. I am a real, genuine person. I may be a pastor, but I'm a human being just like everyone else. I make sure to keep my personal wants, needs, and desires within gauge and occasionally getaway to get in touch with myself. There are times when I have to get away from everyone and everything and take off every title: mother, wife, pastor, friend, etc. I just have to do things that I enjoy and not worry about anyone else. This is what brings everything full circle. I accommodate others when necessary, but then take off the titles and hats at the end of the day so that I can indulge in the personal activities and things I enjoy for myself. I've learned to not lose sight of me amidst the many responsibilities. Why? Because at the end of the day, my children will grow up and leave me, my husband could leave me, the church members could leave and go their separate ways, and the only person I'll have to look after is me. I won't be pastor, wife, mother, friend, etc.; I'll simply be the person I was before I was any of these things: Nikki. So I make sure not to lose sight of myself by doing the things I enjoy doing from time to time.

If you wear multiple hats, I want to encourage you to take some time to get to know yourself if you haven't done so already. Who are you without the title(s) and the position(s)? What do you enjoy doing for you? What are your likes and dislikes? There are so many people in this world who can't even answer those simple questions? They've completely lost sight of themselves. Some people, due to not knowing who

Chapter 3: It's Complicated

they are, have begun to depend too much on their domestic and professional roles and titles to give them an identity and provide them with a sense of belonging. Some people will lean too much on their role as a pastor to compensate for the fact that their personal lives are spiraling out of control. Your kids won't be pastored by you; that will only make them rebel against you more. They want to be loved by you and connect with you outside of the role of pastor. Some pastors defer to home more than they do the work of the ministry because they have a hard time running their ministries due to a lack of setting boundaries and ministering God's Word. Some will become workaholics to escape their failing homes while others will overcompensate with their homes to make up for their lack of success at work. There must be a balance in everything—not too much work, not too much time spent at home, not too much parenting, and not too much befriending. Find your balance. Most importantly, at the end of the day, find yourself. After all, once all else is gone, you're the only one you're going to have to live with and face.

Key Points

- Set boundaries in your life and ministry and stick with them.
- Respect the anointing that's on your life and teach others the importance of respecting the anointing of God as well.
- Understand the responsibility of leadership - that as a leader, your actions have a greater affect on people. So use your influence as a leader the wise way and avoid doing that which causes others to stumble in their faith.
- Take time out to study each role you operate in (mother, father, husband, wife, child, boss, ministry leader, etc.). Learn the differences, duties, and responsibilities associated with each role.
- Pray and ask the Holy Spirit to guide you on how to handle each situation that arises in your life. Each situation is different and may require a different method and call for you to wear a different *hat*.

4 | Auvi

Just A Little Respect

As a PK, one of the biggest challenges I've faced is earning respect from the members of my parents' church. I see myself as my own individual, as a unique person. I have a name, but there are certain times when people in my parents' church will decide not to acknowledge me by my name. This has been a source of frustration for me. It's always frustrating when people act as if you're invisible or they address you like you don't have a name.

Early on in life, PKs discover that they're living in their parents' shadows. Whenever I would be addressed by

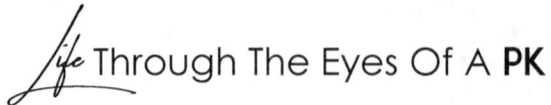
Through The Eyes Of A PK

many members of my parents' church, they'd say things like "Hey, little Nikki" or "Hey, Pastor Nikki's daughter." Rarely would I hear someone say, "Hello, Auvi." To some people, it's as if *Auvi* doesn't exist. If I do good, it's *'Little Nikki did well today.'* If I do something wrong, it's *'The Pastor's daughter messed up today.'*

As time progressed and I got older, whenever people would come up to me and call me Little Nikki, I would correct them by saying kindly, "Just call me Auvi." Some people would respect my wishes, but there were others who felt like they knew me too well to respect my wishes since they saw me grow up around the church or were close to my mom. They'd say things like "Well, I know you as Little Nikki, so I'm just going to keep calling you Little Nikki." It doesn't matter that I'm not little anymore and that my name isn't even Nikki - it's Auvi! They just don't want to respect me as an individual.

I realize that some people don't care that much about a name or a title, but to me these things are important. During slavery in America, one of the ways slave masters humiliated and dehumanized their slaves was by stripping them of their names. By doing this, it left the slaves feeling as if they didn't possess an identity - their identities were assigned to them by their masters. This left them with no sense of pride. A name is powerful; it's how we distinguish between people; it's how we identify others. When we refuse to call a person by his or her name, that is a sign that we don't respect them.

Do you remember when Muhammad Ali beat up Ernie Terrell for calling him out his name? Ali changed his name to Muhammad Ali from Cassius Clay because he didn't want to be acknowledged by his "slave name." Terrell decided to

Chapter 4: Just A Little Respect

call Ali "Cassius Clay" during their weigh-in in a display of disrespect. Ali set out on a mission to beat some respect into Terrell during that fight, which he did. While pounding Terrell's face in, Ali kept shouting and asking him, "What's my name?!!" He'd beat on Terrell some more and then holler, "What's my name?!!" I'm not going to lie to you, there have been times when I felt like knocking some sense into some people's heads while hollering, "What's my name?!! It's Auvi, not Little Nikki!!" But, of course, I'd never go that far. I did, however, develop an *I Don't Care* attitude—and by that, I mean I stopped caring about how I made others feel. I no longer cared if they liked me or not, especially after going off on them and setting them straight. I didn't care about what they thought about my lifestyle. I figured that if they didn't respect me enough to care to acknowledge me by my name, then I needed not care about their feelings while dealing with them. To receive respect you must first give it.

    Much of my rebellious and wild behavior was due to the fact that I was just trying to find myself and establish my own identity. I didn't want the people in the church looking at me as if they owned and controlled me. When I started acting defensively, some people began looking at me as if I was stuck-up and arrogant and didn't want to speak to them. *Nah, boo. It's not that I don't want to speak to you. It's just that if you can't talk to me with respect and treat me like an individual, I don't have anything to say to you.* Yes, I had to go there with several people. I had to state my position and remind some people that my name was not "Pastor Nikki's daughter" or "Little Nikki"—it's Auvi! *Hello! Get to know me!* But the one thing that I've always made it a point of doing is represent-

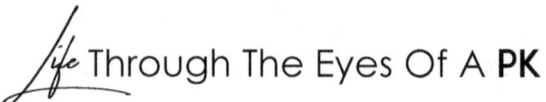 Through The Eyes Of A **PK**

ing my mother well both inside and outside of the church. Regardless of how mad some people may have made me in the church, I'd always think about how my actions would affect my mom. I didn't want to embarrass her. I didn't want to cause her heart unnecessary suffering.

HOW TO DEAL WITH IT

When dealing with disrespect, you can either get bitter or get better. I hate to say this, but not everyone is going to respect you. You can try your best to live up to people's standards and that will never be good enough for them. You can do your best to earn the respect of others and some will never give you the respect that you deserve. That's life.

The truth of the matter is whenever someone disrespects you it's because they lack character. Whenever someone shows disrespect to another, that is usually a sign that they are wrestling with self-esteem issues. For example, bullies have been bullied at one time in their lives. They look for people they can take advantage of and mistreat only because they're still carrying the hurt and pain in their hearts from being mistreated and taken advantage of.

People who feel comfortable disrespecting others lack self-respect and need someone they believe they can take advantage of in order to feel empowered. When you possess confidence in who you are, you don't feel the need to take

Chapter 4: Just A Little Respect

advantage of others.

Don't allow how others treat you to cause you to feel as if you're unworthy of respect and like you're less of an individual. You're no less than anyone else. No one else is better than you. There are no superior human beings. Don't allow yourself to feel as if you are inferior and need another person's validation just to feel important, especially considering the fact that they have their own issues. When they show you disrespect just move on and ignore them. You have nothing to prove.

Just Like Jesus

So you think you have it hard, but Jesus went through it even worse than you. Jesus had to deal with disrespect every day. For example, people didn't want to acknowledge that He was the Son of God. Jesus asked His disciples, "Who do men say that I am?" Peter responded,

"Some say you are a good teacher. Some say you're a good prophet. Some say you're the Prophet Elijah." Then Jesus asked them,

"Who do you say I am?" Peter then answered,

"You're the Son of God."

There Jesus was - the Son of God, God wrapped up in human flesh, the one who performed miracles such as healing the sick and raising the dead - dealing with disrespect from the very people He was blessing. People didn't want to acknowledge Him according to who He was. They wanted His blessings, but they didn't want to honor Him. Sadly, later on, many of those same people began chanting, "Crucify Him!" while He was on trial. *That's cold!*

Life Through The Eyes Of A **PK**

People are fickle. They'll turn on you. They'll change. One minute they like you and the next minute they dislike you. One minute they're on your side and the next minute they're fighting against you alongside your enemies. You can't base your self-esteem and self-worth on the opinions of others. If people have the audacity to disrespect God, they'll certainly disrespect you without a cause.

> " Don't allow how others treat you to cause you to feel as if you're unworthy of respect and like you're less of an individual. You're no less than anyone else. No one else is better than you. "

To be honest, all of us occasionally engage in behaviors deemed disrespectful. You may not have cursed someone out or stolen something from your neighbor or anything like that, but you probably neglected to thank God this morning for the breath He gave you. You may have neglected to thank God for His many blessings before begging Him for new blessings. I bet you've misrepresented God in many ways, doing things that bring shame to Him throughout the day. This, too, is considered a form of disrespect.

When we think about what God has to put up with from us on a daily basis, this reminds us to be loving, patient,

Chapter 4: Just A Little Respect

kind and forgiving towards those who mistreat us. If God forgives us, we must forgive others. We should treat others the way God treats us.

BOUNDARIES

Just because you forgive someone for being disrespectful towards you, that doesn't mean you have to allow that person to continue to disrespect you. Continue to set boundaries. By this, you teach people to respect you. By boundaries, I'm not talking about controlling other people; I'm talking about controlling yourself and determining what you respond to.

For example, if someone wrongly addresses me, I'll kindly express to them how I want to be addressed. If that person chooses to continue to address me the wrong way, I'll ignore them and refuse to answer them. By doing this, I am communicating to them that I don't approve of the name they're calling me. I'll voice to them my disapproval and let them know that the door of communication between us won't be reopened until they show me the proper respect. Furthermore, I know that the Holy Spirit can do what I can't do, so I'll pray for those who have an issue with showing respect to me and my family. I'll ask the Holy Spirit to melt their hearts and move in their lives. And while praying for them, I also pray for God to move in my heart and life and make sure that I'm not walking in error and harboring offense.

Don't run from your place of destiny just because there are people there who don't like you. That's where you belong. Don't let them drive you away. You stay put and let them leave. Do what God called you to do. Be the man or woman God called you to be. Be confident in the person God made you. Don't run from God and the church because of someone else who has the same problems you have. Just as God sent the Israelites into the Land of Canaan where there were giants waiting for them, there are giants in the land that God predestined for you to dwell in. That's commonplace. Just like the Israelites, God has given you the power to defeat every giant in your path. When you're where you belong, nothing will be able to defeat you nor stop you. Discover who you are and walk in it.

> When we think about what God has to put up with from us on a daily basis, this reminds us to be loving, patient, kind and forgiving towards those who mistreat us. If God forgives us, we must forgive others. We should treat others the way God treats us.

RESPECT IN MINISTRY

I'll be honest and admit that there were times when my mom had to get on me for doing or saying things that were out of line. I may have gotten too friendly with her and forgot that she was in pastor-mode, or forgot that above all else she was still my mom. Of course, once I would receive that look from her, I knew I was doing too much.

Adjusting to the many roles my mom has to fill has

Chapter 4: Just A Little Respect

been a learning experience for me, too. But all relationships thrive off of such continual learning. You can be married to someone for forty or fifty years and still find yourself discovering new things about them. We never stop learning. The moment we stop taking time to get to know one another, that's when we'll begin to take one another for granted.

The thing that helps my mother and I work well together is the fact that I know how to respect her and not take her for granted. I see my mom as a unique, distinct individual who deserves my utmost respect. If I am careful not to cross my friends' boundaries, then why would I feel entitled to cross my family members' boundaries, especially my mom's? Understanding the importance of respect and knowing what true friendship is is what prevents me from overstepping boundaries and helps me to get back in line if and when I do.

I don't believe in using people. That's a personal, moral defect. When we use, misuse, and abuse people, that's because we personally lack integrity, self-respect, and a positive self-esteem. My ability to respect my mom begins with my awareness of who I am…and whose I am. Knowing who I am makes it easier for me to not feel as if submitting to another is a way of degrading or cheapening myself. Yes, I can submit with confidence to authority because I know that submission is an act of my will, not someone else's. I submit out of love and because I choose to, realizing the blessings that come as a result of submitting to authority. I am empowered by this knowledge and enjoy serving because I know that Jesus was a servant and that the way to elevation is humility according to the Word of God. Every opportunity that I get to serve is a blessing because it allows me to sow seeds that will come back

to bless me later on.

I show respect to my parents around the church by acknowledging them according to their titles and positions. I don't say, "Mom!" when around the church; instead, I refer to her as "Pastor". By doing this, I'm training the members of the church to respect her position and authority. I realize that when my mom is in front of members and when she's in certain settings, she's "Pastor". When she's at home, she's "mom".

> Every opportunity that I get to serve is a blessing because it allows me to sow seeds that will come back to bless me later on.

By showing respect to my mom, it has not only caused her to appreciate me even more, but it also causes others to gain more respect for me as well. Believe it or not, but your display of respect for authority actually motivates and inspires others within your church or organization. They may never tell you, but they're watching you and are very moved by the fact that you know how to adjust to the many hats your loved-one(s) wear. This will open doors for you as an individual. When people see your loyalty and respect for authority, they'll feel comfortable with blessing you with opportunities. It all goes back to what Jesus said in the Gospel of Luke 16:12 which says,

> "And if you have not been faithful in that which is another's, who will give you that which is your own?" (ESV)

Chapter 4: Just A Little Respect

Faithfulness opens doors and causes others to be impressed with you and trust you. Most of all, your faithfulness to those God has placed as authority figures in your life will cause God to open up doors for you and one-day place you in a position of authority. So don't run from your assignment, fellow PK. Stay true to God, to who you are, to your calling, forgive others and serve where God has planted you. Oh, and let God deal with your haters.

Key Points

- Don't take other people's disrespect personally. Realize that they have the problem, not you.
- Set boundaries for how other people may treat you and behave around you.
- Don't try to live up to everyone else's expectations. Just focus on living up to God's expectations and honoring and respecting your own parents.
- Remember to forgive others just as God has forgiven you.
- Never take those close to you for granted.
- Realize that only through becoming a servant can you be elevated by God. By serving others you are sowing seeds of blessings that will return to you up the road.
- Let love be your only motivation for serving others.

5 | Pastor Nikki & Auvi

Overcoming Stereotypes

(Pastor Nikki)

If you're serving in a position of leadership in any organization, it is important that you not allow people to place you in a box and try to shape you into what they want you to be. That's a natural tendency of people. Everyone has an opinion and will make you become what he or she wants you to be if you let them. I'm not exempt from this. There are times when I have to remind myself that although I'm my kid's mother, I'm not their God. I can only do so much in their lives. I can't protect them from every storm. I can't make their decisions for them. I can't determine their futures.

Life Through The Eyes Of A PK

All I can do is train them to pray and seek God for themselves so that He can protect and guide them. God may have given them to me to raise, but ultimately He created them for Himself to serve His will (Proverbs 16; Ephesians 2). I'm just a vessel being used by God to pour into their lives. But in spite of knowing this, even I face the temptation to play God in my children's lives and try to shape them into what I want them to be.

As your children grow up, they will make decisions for themselves. Some of the decisions they make will please you and some of them will trouble you. It doesn't matter how much you pour into them and teach them what's right, they'll still make mistakes from time to time and do what they want to do. Like I shared with my daughter, I've been where she is in many respects. I know what she likes. I've been there in many ways. I'll never forget one time the two of us were at one of my son's basketball game. While we were sitting in the bleachers, a boy came up to Auvi and tried to talk to her. I could tell Auvi wasn't feeling him, and plus he was kind of rude in that he acted like he didn't see me sitting there. After Auvi checked him, the boy left. Auvi and I turned and stared at each other, and then I said to her, "Yeah, I already knew you weren't feeling him anyway because that's not your type."

"Mom, what are you talking about?"
"I know you. I know your type."
"How do you know my type?"
"Because I was you. He wasn't your type. Who you really want is that boy at the entrance of the building with those dreads in his hair. That's your type."

Chapter 5: Overcoming Stereotypes

"Mom!" Auvi said, shocked. "How did you know I was checking him out?"

"Because you're me," I replied.

As parents, we know our children. We know what they're thinking most of the times, how they're feeling, what they want, how they'll react and respond in certain situations, and what challenges often lie ahead of them. Why? Because they carry our DNA. They came from us. We know how we were when we were their ages.

Don't act shocked that your daughter may be dating a bad boy. When you were her age, that's what you were into. So, stop acting like you were a perfect angel that only focused on hitting the books. I admit that I was a mess when I was younger. I was part of a neighborhood gang, trafficked cocaine, sold dope, hung with hustlers, married a drug dealer, did everything I felt like I was big and bad enough to do, fought everyone, and drove my mother crazy. So I can't look at my children funny because they face many of the same temptations I faced and even act in ways similar to the way I acted when I was their age. The only difference between me back then and my children today is I didn't have parents who taught me the Word of God. My parents weren't into church. My children have a mother who teaches them the Word of God so that they can know the truth and make wise decisions. Had I known the truth about sin, about God, about heaven and hell, and gained an understanding of my true purpose and identity in Christ when I was younger, I might have made better decisions in my life back then.

As much as we know our kids, we don't know everything about them. They are still individuals with their own minds. They can make decisions that completely baffle us. Sometimes they'll shock us with who they choose to date and marry. Sometimes they'll fall into traps we ourselves never experienced. Sometimes they'll get involved in things we know nothing about and we'll find ourselves clueless on how to guide them. Remember, God told us in Ezekiel chapter 18 that every person is responsible for their own sins. God said if the father does right and the child does wrong, the father will be blessed and the child will be cursed, and vice-versa. God even began that passage of Scripture by saying, "No longer will this proverb be used in the land: The fathers have eaten sour grapes and the children's teeth have come out rotten." That's powerful because it suggests to us that we're all individuals who make our own choices; that we're not, as some scientists may claim, preprogrammed to do what our physical natures tell us to do. <u>Just because I may carry my parents' DNA, that doesn't mean my actions are predetermined; it doesn't mean I'm going to automatically do what my parents did and live how they lived. I choose my actions.</u>

We love to use the excuse *'I'm this way because my parents were this way,'* but that doesn't justify our wrongdoings. If our parents lived a certain lifestyle, we still have a choice in the matter of how we're going to live. If your parents ate nothing but fried foods and ended up with high blood pressure and sugar diabetes because of their poor diet, that doesn't mean you have to end up with the same medical conditions. You can break the curse and be healthy. I've seen children surpass their parents in many ways, choosing not to follow in their parents' footsteps. We all make our own choices in life and must deal with the consequences. So no one can be God

Chapter 5: Overcoming Stereotypes

in another person's life.

Just as parents tend to think they know everything about their children and will often try to control their lives, people tend to do the same to leaders. I have encountered members of my church who felt like it was their responsibility to mold me into the person they think I should be. I've dealt with peers in the ministry who took it upon themselves to try to mold me into what they thought I should be.

Like I explained in the introduction of this book, I face many challenges in ministry. One of the biggest challenges I face is being a female pastor. I hate to admit it, but women aren't necessarily welcomed in every pulpit. In fact, many churches and Christian denominations don't allow women to preach at all. I still get funny stares from people when I tell them that I'm a pastor of a church. Some of them look at me as if I'm doing something wrong, and as if I'm out of place. In some churches where I've preached, when they'd announce that I (a woman) was preaching, I'd notice the men sizing me up because I'm a woman preacher, but I never allowed their faces to move me. They'd size me up because I'm a woman, not because I was walking in error doctrinally. Some men couldn't bring themselves to receive from a woman. This tradition is breaking in many churches and even denominations today, but things are still tough for women. <u>I'm thankful that I am no longer bound by gender stereotypes. I love to watch God destroy gender barriers and deliver His people as I obey Him while on my ministry assignment.</u>

Some people told me that I needed a husband in order to pastor a church. (After the death of my first husband, I was still pastoring the church we started.) This was expected of

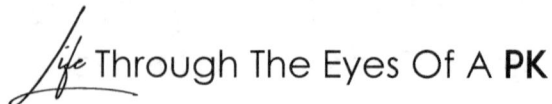

me by several of my Christian colleagues, but I couldn't put God's assignment for me on hold just to please a couple of people who were bound by man-made traditions. Jesus didn't!

If I had to live my life based off of the expectations of people, I would not be in the ministry today. Instead, I'd simply be a cute First Lady sitting on the side wearing a big hat, a fancy suit, and looking like an accessory on a man's arm. I wouldn't be operating in the role of a pastor. I wouldn't be sharing my testimony with others, winning lost souls for the Kingdom of God, and doing what God called me to do.

Not only did I have to face a crowd that didn't welcome women preachers, but I also had to deal with a religious crowd that believes women preachers must look a certain way. Many of my Christian peers stress the importance of dressing very modestly and avoiding looking "worldly." I've come to discover, however, that God has a definition of "worldliness" that differs from what many religious people call worldly. "Worldliness" to God means *living according to the dictates of our sinful flesh; acting independently of God's Spirit and operating outside of His Word*. We should pray about everything and seek God's wisdom, counsel, and guidance in every situation (Proverbs 3:5-6). But to religious people, "worldliness" means breaking man-made traditions and rules that have only been established to give men control over others. This has nothing to do with God. In a strict, religious environment, women are discouraged and even prohibited from wearing jeans, they can't wear makeup, they can't put color in their hair or wear certain hairstyles, they can't wear fitted clothing; they have to wear big, fancy hats; they have to wear suits and dresses that make them look old, and they have to fellowship

Chapter 5: Overcoming Stereotypes

with certain cliques and attend certain social functions. All of this hit me the moment I joined the ministry. I was faced with a ton of do's and don't's.

I don't have a problem with certain rules. I understand some of them and why they're in place, and I agree with many of them. I understand the importance of modesty. I mean, today's women will show up in church practically naked. There has to be a level of respectability. You won't show up to court looking any old way, so why treat God's house with a lack of respect. So, yes, there are some rules that need to be acknowledged.

> "'Worldliness' to God means *living according to the dictates of our sinful flesh; acting independently of God's Spirit and operating outside of His Word.*"

But when it comes to the heart of God, we must always weigh what is more important to God: the outer appearance or the soul? God is concerned more with where your soul is going than He is with where you buy the latest fashions. As the old saying goes: *You can't clean a fish until you first catch it*. And you can't win souls with religion. It takes the love and power of God to draw the lost. Knowing this, I endeavored to make my church one where all people will feel welcomed. I didn't want my church to be religiously bound. I don't care if people show up to my church with jeans and tennis shoes on. It doesn't matter if your hair is fixed or not. I fix my hair up. I wear color in my hair. One day, I might have blonde in my hair, and then purple and grey in it the next; burgundy in it after that. That alone is uncustomary among many ministry circles. Basically, I don't look like what many people expressed to me that a pastor is supposed to look like. Some days I'll preach in jeans and sometimes I'll preach in a beautiful dress or a suit. You never know. I believe in being unconventional because Jesus was unconventional. Jesus didn't treat women with contempt and as inferior. He instead allowed women to accompany Him while He traveled around preaching and performing miracles, which was uncustomary for a Jewish rabbi. Many of His followers were women. He allowed His disciples to pick wheat on the Sabbath day, which was uncustomary. He healed people on the Sabbath day, which was outlawed by the Pharisees. He went into the Samaritan's territory, which no Jew would ever do out of fear of public ridicule and shame. He ate with tax collectors and sinners, which the religious people tried to shame Him for. He allowed a prostitute to wash His feet with her hair, which the Pharisees criticized Him for. Basically, everything about Jesus' ministry was non-traditional, unconventional, and radical.

The Apostle Paul told us in Colossians 2:16-17,

> "So don't let anyone condemn you for what you eat or drink, or for not celebrating certain holy days or new moon ceremonies or Sabbaths. For these rules are only shadows of the reality to come. And Christ himself is that reality."

Christianity is not a set of rituals, it is a relationship with God. We're not saved because we attend church; we're saved because we've accepted Jesus' atonement for our sins and have

Chapter 5: Overcoming Stereotypes

developed a genuine relationship with Him. Going to church helps us in our Christian walk, but it doesn't define us as Christians. We're Christians because we love God and obey His commandments.

I choose not to conform to rules that will hinder the work of the Holy Spirit in my ministry. The lost aren't coming to church to be pounded with a bunch of condemnation over the way they look. Even if a young woman comes to the church half naked, my goal is to love her, not to condemn her. She didn't have to show up. If she's there it's because she wants to change; she wants to know God. Since souls are perishing every day without God, I can't be concerned with trying to fit in with a Christian country club. God didn't call me to a denomination, He called me to the vineyard to bring lost souls into His Kingdom. This is the thing I have to remind myself of every day. When it comes down to living according to man's expectations or God expectations, man must take the backseat.

> Christianity is not a set of rituals; it is a relationship with God.

(Auvi)

As a PK, I face expectations all of the time. People expect my siblings and I to be perfect. They expect us to never make mistakes, be sinless, get straight A's in all of our classes in school, have perfect conduct and attendance, have pearly white teeth, starched clothes, pressed hair, perfect bodies, perfectly clean

Life Through The Eyes Of A PK

rooms at home, perfect faith, know every book in the Bible, know every verse in the Bible; possess super-human strength, speed, and ability; be able to fly and shoot gamma rays from our eyes, etc.

Growing up, there were times when I'd go to parties and notice a few of the youth from my church present, but for whatever reason, everyone would make a big deal out of me being there. Whenever I'd do something wrong, even if all of the other kids from my church were doing it, everyone would come down on my head like a hailstorm while saying nothing to the other kids.

I discovered that when you're a PK, people hold you to a higher standard than everyone else and they tend to expect perfection from you. PKs usually run from this and avoid church altogether or they might cave in and attempt to conform; most run away from the church. I've known PKs to move to another state just to get away from the people in the churches they grew up in. I've seen PKs develop a hatred of authority and rules due to the pressure placed on them by churchgoers to be exceptional and perfect. Many of these PKs have grown sick of the double-standards practiced by many church people. It's not that these PKs hate God, it's just that they don't like church.

Gandhi once stated, "If it weren't for Christians, I'd be a Christian." He was one of the greatest and most well-respected revolutionaries in world history. He led the people of India in a non-violent revolt against the British Empire who was oppressing them. Gandhi was a Hindu, but He was fascinated with Jesus and the Bible. In spite of all of that, the thing that prevented him from embracing the Christian faith was

Chapter 5: Overcoming Stereotypes

the horrible example of Christianity set by those who claim to be Christians.

Just like Gandhi, there are many people, especially PKs, that have been turned off by the church. Many PKs are turned off by their parents' churches. Some PKs will attend other churches before they attend their parents' churches. In general, many young people are turned off by the church because of the double-standards imposed on them by many churchgoers. For example, some within the older generation will look down on the youth because of their mistakes rather than show them compassion and offer them advice in a loving manner. They'll forget that they made the same mistakes when they were younger. The older generations smoked weed, slept around, partied, clubbed, and did things their parents didn't approve of also. They were once young. The crazy thing is, all they were looking for was their own identities as individuals; they just wanted the freedom to be themselves. When many of these same individuals look at the youth today, they look at them with judgmental eyes and try to shame them. It's as if they expect the youth to be better, I mean, *perfect* versions of themselves. Many want to live vicariously through and correct their mistakes in the lives of the youth.

Yes, we should avoid doing wrong. Yes, we should learn from the mistakes of the past, but the problem with the church today isn't the abundance of mistakes, it's the absence of love. Rather than talk about that young girl who messed up or is messing up, pray for her. Turn your gossip sessions into a prayer session and then love her into wholeness. She needs and wants your guidance, but she doesn't need your condemnation of her. Her soul is precious to God also.

Life Through The Eyes Of A PK

A judgmental attitude is what causes the youth to leave the church, even while still seeking after God. This is what causes so many young people to identify with other religions today despite growing up in Christian households: they want God, but they don't like church people. When this happens, Islam, Buddhism, Hinduism, Wicca, etc. is there to offer these young people love and acceptance.

Some pastors have noticed the dilemna young Christians are facing today and they have began capitalizing on it. Young people who feel judged and rejected by the older generations of churchgoers are hungry for God just like everyone

> **But the problem with the church today isn't the abundance of mistakes, it's the absence of love. Rather than talk about that young girl who messed up or is messing up, pray for her. Turn your gossip sessions into a prayer session. And then love her into wholeness.**

else, but they also want to feel loved, accepted, and welcomed. Seeing this, some pastors have now designed their ministries to appeal to this particular group. These pastors don't impose strict dress codes, put people down from the pulpits, act as if

Chapter 5: Overcoming Stereotypes

they're better than others, and attempt to hide their own past and mistakes. They're much more transparent, knowing that this generation craves truth and transparency. Our motto is: *Don't approach us like you've lived a perfect life. Don't talk to us like we don't know anything. Don't try to transform us by force. Instead, show us the love of God and let the Word do the work of transforming our hearts.*

If you're a pastor and your child is comfortable with attending another church besides yours, then you have to decide which is more important in the situation: your child attending a different church or your child turning away from the church altogether because they can't stand being under the pressure the members of your church place on them? Essentially, the real question here is are you concerned about your child's soul or about your image and ego as a pastor? If they're in a good church, praise God for that. At least they're still in a place where they can hear the Word of God.

As I mentioned earlier, the only thing that caused me to want to serve in my parents' ministry despite all of the unfair and hypocritical expectations thrown on me by others in the church is my love and respect for my parents and my love and respect for God. If my mom didn't take the time to build a healthy relationship with me, I probably wouldn't be working alongside her in the ministry. I certainly wouldn't have put up with all of the hypocritical expectations and disrespect from others. But what I learned how to do is remain loyal to my mom and the Lord. I don't hold myself to anyone else's expectations besides God's and my parents'.

One thing that I love about my mom—the thing that strengthened the bond between us even more—is that when

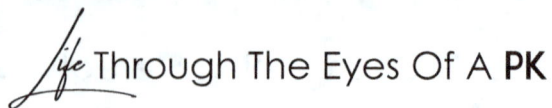# Through The Eyes Of A PK

people would approach her with some accusation against me for something I did or they claim I did, she would never simply take their side and then attack me alongside them just to impress them. Some pastors will side with their members against their own children just to appear to be unbiased, and yet, they'll show favoritism towards the members. My mom wasn't having that. She wasn't going to allow anyone to divide our family and turn us against one another. If someone stepped to her and tried to turn her against me, she'd check them real quick even if that meant losing them as a member.

As a family, one thing we always maintained was the fact that church members often come and go, but the family remains the same. If you allow a member of your church to turn you against your own family members, after the damage has been done that member will most likely end up leaving your church anyway, but you'll be the one that's left picking up the pieces of a shattered family. If I did something wrong, my mom wouldn't allow the members to chastise me. She would establish boundaries that they couldn't cross when it came to our family.

> When families are torn apart, that's when the children involved become susceptible to the outside pressures placed on them.

Having a close-knit, strong and loving family protected my siblings and me from the outside pressures and expectations of others. Our family was the main source of strength and identity for us; it was the place where we became grounded, and it's because of this we didn't feel the need to be what

Chapter 5: Overcoming Stereotypes

others expected us to be just to gain their approval.

    When families are torn apart, that's when the children involved become susceptible to the outside pressures placed on them. Sadly, there are so many First Families out here that are emotionally disconnected. They fake it in church while behind closed doors, they don't even talk to one another. That's a recipe for disaster. Don't be so concerned about appearing to be a strong family while overlooking how dysfunctional you are as a family privately.

Life Through The Eyes Of A PK

Key Points

- Pray for your children rather than attempting to control them.
- Prioritize your home above the church. Taking care of home is an act of serving God.
- Let your children make their own decisions in life, this includes mistakes. They must learn on their own.
- Focus on your mission and not people's rejection. (Remember: they rejected Jesus, too.)
- Don't get trapped in religion. Focus on developing a relationship with Christ and winning the lost.
- Rather than be judgmental of others, show compassion and love and pray for them when they are in error.
- People will be willing to receive correction and rebuke when they first feel loved and accepted.
- Strengthening your relationship with your children will protect them from outside influences.

6 | Auvi

Lessons From My Parents

As I watched my mom throughout the years as she served faithfully in the ministry, many of the lessons she taught me she did so without ever saying a word. I watched her example and learned how to handle some tough situations.

While serving as a single parent, I watched my mom struggle to hold the family together and hold down the ministry. She had to do it all on her own, and not only that, but she had to manage all of this while still grieving as a widow. She was still healing emotionally while helping others to heal.

Life Through The Eyes Of A **PK**

She didn't have an opportunity to be vulnerable because both her family and church depended on her. She never really had an opportunity to slow down. What amazes me is in the midst of this she never missed a beat when it came to investing in her kids. She never substituted being a mother with being a pastor. She never neglected us physically, mentally, and emotionally.

What I learned from my mom is the importance of family and how to value family above all else while keeping the ministry and other ventures in proper perspective. I learned how to balance myself while juggling multiple roles and responsibilities.

Another thing I learned from my mom is that leadership is not about controlling and manipulating others, it's about controlling your actions despite what others may do and say to you. This is the example of leadership she set throughout her life and ministry. Regardless of what others say and do to you, it's important that you maintain a sense of self-control and regulate your words and actions. Carry yourself with dignity even while others may be acting foolish. Climb higher when people are trying to pull you down to where they are.

Lesson #1

What I learned from my mom is the importance of family and how to value family above all else while keeping the ministry and other ventures in proper perspective.

One of the hardest things for me to witness was my mom being disrespected by others in the church. She'd bite

Chapter 6: Lessons From My Parents

her lip, grit her teeth, and hold her tongue when she wanted to retaliate. She had to practice restraint and self-control because she understood the price of leadership. Like any ministry or organization, there are people who'll get angry with the leader for whatever reason. But some disgruntled members or employees, rather than leaving, will hang around and sow the seeds of discord in that church or organization in order to destroy it from within. They aren't looking for another place to worship; they're looking for a place they can tear down.

My mom might have admonished a member of the church for whatever reason—and one thing that I've discovered is that not everyone can take correction—and as a result of being rebuked, that person will become bitter and defensive and try to retaliate against her by telling lies, spreading false rumors, and doing and saying other rude things to her in order to get her to lose her cool publicly. I've witnessed these things being done to my mom by people she trusted, by people she helped personally when they were in need, by people whose bills she paid using her own money, by people she prayed for in the midnight hours, by people she rushed to the hospital to stand beside when they were suffering, by people I thought would never turn their backs on her. I have seen my mom make personal sacrifices for people who later ran her name through the mud because they couldn't have their way in the church.

Witnessing this type of activity has shaped my perspective greatly. I don't get excited when people come up to my mom and I and profess how much they love us and support us. I don't fall gullible to people's praises because I've seen people praise my mom one day and then curse her the next. I've seen so many people come and go that it no longer moves me. I've seen people get excited in the beginning and then fizzle out in the end. Yes, people can be very fickle. Some members are only seasonal. Some people mean well, but unforeseen circumstances can arise and pull them away (job relocations, family tragedies, etc.).

Helping people without having any strings attached is something I witnessed my mom do. She's been around for a while and knows the ropes. She understands more than me how people can be. She's experienced the betrayal, the back-stabbing and back-biting, and she knows that when she helps someone there's a possibility that that person may never return the favor. That's why my mom is so willing to help others without looking for anything from them in return.

In the Bible, God warns us many times against helping people with strings attached. Matthew 6:3 tells us to give without letting our "left hand know what your right hand is doing." This means we're not even supposed to keep a record of all of the things we've done for others. When we bless others, we're to move on and forget about the good we've done rather than keep a track-record of it and build a monument to it. Luke 6:38 tells us to "give, and it will be given to you. Good measure, pressed down, shaken together, running over, will be put into your lap. For with the measure you

> **Lesson #2**
>
> Leadership is not about controlling and manipulating others, it's about controlling your actions despite what others may do and say to you.

Chapter 6: Lessons From My Parents

use it will be measured back to you" (ESV). God promises us here that when we show kindness towards others, that kindness will be returned unto us. But He never said we'd reap kindness from the people we showed it to; He just said it will come back to us in a greater measure. Sometimes you may do something kind for one person and end up being blessed by someone completely different, a stranger even, in return.

Lastly, Proverbs 19:17 says, "Whoever is generous to the poor lends to the LORD, and he will repay him for his deed" (ESV). Notice here that God says when you bless others who are less fortunate you are serving Him, and He promises to repay you for the things you have done to help others. Your reward comes from God, not from people. This is what God says to us in Colossians 3:23-24 where He says, "And whatsoever ye do, do it heartily, as to the Lord, and not unto men; knowing that of the Lord ye shall receive the reward of the inheritance: for ye serve the Lord Christ."

<u>We're not supposed to look for people to repay us for the good we've done. God told us He'll repay us for the good we do unto others. In fact, if we do good for others without looking for them to return to us a favor, that's when God steps in and repays us.</u> On the other hand, if we help and serve others with strings attached, God will not reward us for the things we've done because they were done out of selfish motives.

Despite the many people that have stabbed my mom in the back, I've continued to watch her get blessed and prosper day after day. God keeps on blessing her. The reason for this is she refuses to allow the pain of abandonment and betrayal to make her bitter and cause her to stop sowing seeds of generosity in the lives of others; after all, that's what bitterness does: it causes us to close up our hearts for fear of being hurt and stop doing kind things for others. One of my mom's greatest strengths is her ability to forgive and continue to bless others without worrying about whether or not they'll bless her back. Her example has inspired me in so many ways and helped me to deal with the negative things done to me by others.

As a leader, you have to protect your heart from bitterness. Bitterness will kill your joy and happiness and stump your creativity. Bitterness is like a dam holding back the waters of greatness in your life. You can't stop people from doing things to you, but you can prevent your heart from harboring bitterness towards them for the things they've said and done. And the key to overcoming bitterness is remembering from whom your blessings come. As long as you remember that God is the source of your blessings, your joy, your peace and the strength of your life, you'll never make the mistake of putting so much hope in men.

Both my mom and my late father, Adrian Canady, lived by the creed: *Your word is your bond*. They believed in integrity more than anything. If you say you're going to do something, do it. If you promise someone something, deliver on it. The one thing that will destroy your career, ministry, and life is making promises you can't or won't keep

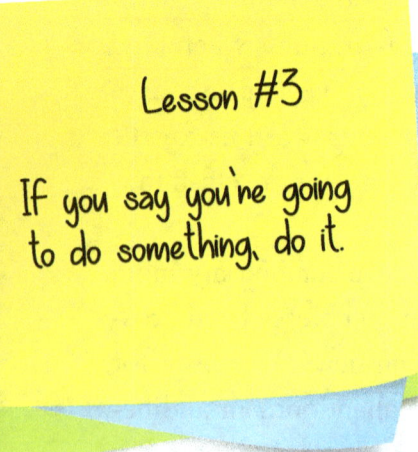

Lesson #3

If you say you're going to do something, do it.

Chapter 6: Lessons From My Parents

and falling back on your word. When you become unreliable and undependable, that's when your world will come crashing down.

All you have in life is your word and reputation. This is why Proverbs 221:1 tells us, "Choose a good reputation over great riches; being held in high esteem is better than silver or gold" (NLT). You build a reputation by doing something consistently, which means over and over again the same way. If I go to a restaurant one day and the food is good and then go back the next day and the same dish is seasoned differently and tastes horrible, I'll lose trust in that restaurant because the quality of its food isn't consistent. The same is to be said about everything we do in life.

> As a leader, you have to protect your heart from bitterness.

In the ministry, my mom has to remain consistent in her message and in her delivery of that message. She makes it **her** goal to bring the house down each and every time she gets up to preach. She doesn't slack off in her studying of God's Word, neither does she take for granted the people coming out to hear her. She believes in the power of God moving every week. I've noticed her dedication to what she does, taking note of the fact that she gives it her all every time she gets the opportunity to do so. She's passionate about what she does and does it for the right reasons. This attitude is clearly visible to those who see her and it makes a huge impression on those attending the church.

My mom and dad were real in the streets, and they certainly weren't going to be fake in the church. That's all they know to be. That's what they trained me and my siblings to be. These lessons have become the foundation of my life, guiding my every action. That's what I gleaned from my parents.

Chapter 6: Lessons From My Parents

Key Points

- Prioritize your family above other people.
- As a leader, focus on controlling yourself and not controlling others.
- Help others without having strings attached. When you selflessly bless others, God will bless you in return.
- Don't expect those you help to be the vehicles God return your blessings through.
- Forgive others when they hurt you and keep a clean heart.
- Focus on building and maintaining integrity and a good reputation.
- Be consistent in what you do and do it to the best of your ability.

PASTOR NIKKI'S COMMANDMENTS

THOU SHALL NOT LOOK TO MEMBERS FOR CORRECTION CONCERNING YOUR CHILDREN

THOU SHALL NOT TELL YOUR PERSONAL FAMILY BUSINESS TO YOUR MEMBERS

THOU SHALL NOT BE MORE CONCERNED WITH MINISTRY RELATIONSHIPS THAN FAMILY RELATIONSHIPS

AUVI'S COMMANDMENTS

THOU SHALT NOT COMPARE YOUR KIDS TO OTHER PKS

THOU SHALT NOT PUT MINISTRY BEFORE FAMILY. FAMILY OVER EVERYTHING!

THOU SHALT REMEMBER YOUR FAMILY LEGACY MATTERS

Perspectives FROM TWO GENERATIONS

(Pastor Nikki)

Q: What do you think the church needs to do to reach today's generation with the Gospel?
A: I think the church needs to reach the generation where they are not where they have been!

Q: What does your ideal church look like (music type, decor, dress style, etc.)?
A: Our church is warm, inviting, family oriented, casual, and on fire for God! Our band is like no other. We have live worship music playing each Sunday!

Q: What are the tough issues the church has to deal with today?
A: Helping those in need financially even when they aren't members. We do put a cap on how much we are able to give non members though.

Q: What approach would you take in confronting these issues (ex. a transgender person joins your church; a gay couple joins the church and want to get married; etc.)?
A: We have had transgender people attend the ministry and we show them love and kindness. We also had a gay couple

come often and we loved on them just as Christ would. But had they desired to get married at our church, our bylaws state that according to our beliefs and the scriptural principals, we WOULD NOT have performed any such matrimony.

Q: What is most appealing to you about the Gospel message?
A: Seeing lives transformed! I love when the Word [of God] changes a thug into a Holy Ghost filled man of God, or changes a *thot* into a sanctified, fire-baptized worship leader. I love when the Word [of God] transforms a non-believer!

(Auvi)

Q: What do you think the church needs to do to reach today's generation with the Gospel?
A: Be more relate-able. My generation isn't into the *thou's* and they don't understand that there is nothing new under the sun. Our generation doesn't want words; we want actions.

Q: What does your ideal church look like (music type, decor, dress style, etc.)?
A: Even though I'm young, I still believe in holiness, worship, praise - and a little [Christian] rap is fine. But God still inhabits our worship. And as far as appearances go, I say come as you are.

Q: What are the tough issues the church has to deal with today?

A: Not being judgmental and not understanding that we young people go through just about as much as they do as adults.

Q: What approach would you take in confronting these issues (ex. a transgender person joins your church; a gay couple joins the church and want to get married; etc.)?
A: Well, at Harvest Springs, we have put in our legal paperwork that we won't be officiating gay marriages. So, our answer will remain no - and we have rights to back that.

Q: What is most appealing to you about the Gospel message?
A: People change, but God never changes. I can always count on Him. I can always lean on Him.

(Aumani)

Q: What challenges do you face as a PK?
A: I face the "All Eyes On Me " syndrome. I don't like the fact that people expect you to be a certain way because your parents are pastors. The other challenge is sharing your parents with the church. My final one is seeing church people hurt your parents over and over. You have to sit back and watch them (your parents) be the bigger person.

(Ahmad)

Q: Who's my Christian influencer and why?
A: I choose Tre Davis. I appreciate that he takes time with me to help groom me into a good drummer. I'm thankful that he is patient with me. He influence me because he's young like me. He maintains a positive attitude even when things are challenging for him!

(Alijahuan)

Q: What changes would you like to implement in the church so that it could be more effective in reaching today's generation?
A: I would like to see more youth adding their ideas to events that takes place at the church. I would like to see youth working more in the church. The elders should train us and not push us away.

(Pastor Marvin McQueen, a PK friend)

Being a preacher's (or pastor's) kid is very different from being another "normal" kid. We are sometimes under internal and external pressure. We have had to live in a bubble and on the top shelf only to be seen by everyone. While many experience raising, training, and rearing in various ways, there is a blessing in being who you are. The authority, power, and calling that rest on our parents has a future effect on us. There is a blessing in being in line, in support, and in the position of a pastor's/preacher's kid. We are blessed with learning accountability, responsibility, and solid spiritual maturity. No matter what others may say or do to a pastor's/preacher's kid, we are blessed and able to receive increase in our lives.

ABOUT THE AUTHORS

PASTOR NIKKI CANADY-BOYD is a teacher, preacher, a certified Christian Life Coach, servant, and author who is in love with God Almighty. A native of Jacksonville Florida. At an early age the Lord began to deal with her heavy concerning the call on her life. Running from this call, she chose the fast lifestyle of trafficking, selling, and using drugs.

The Lord made a swift transition within her life, as he called her to marry her high school sweetheart, the late Pastor Adrian L. Canady in January 1993 and they remained as a union until his departure November 2014. Faced with a life altering encounter, Pastor Nikki would carry the ministry that was founded by her and her late husband. After his untimely departure is when she realized it was now time to demonstrate everything she was taught by her mentor and late husband. Pressing beyond the pressure, destined to fulfill the God given purpose is what she is called to do.

While traveling extensively across the country for a number of years, she found her passion for helping young men & women with her similar backgrounds. Pastor Nikki's heart goes out to abused women, young ladies, and teen mothers. Lives have been changed through her ministry as she allows the Lord to unmask her, while sharing real life issues, and relate them to the Word of God allowing deliverance to take place.

Pastor Nikki founded "Spiritual Diaries in the Word" women's ministries, every 3rd Saturday she sets aside this time to hear the heart of the women, have lunch and prepare special outings for them to enjoy each other. Pastor Nikki is currently enrolled in Liberty University where she is pursuing a Bachelor degree in Theology with a minor in Biblical Studies. Pastor Nikki launched the very first Birthing God's Purpose Conference in October 2013 and it continues every other year! October 2015, was the release of Pastor Nikki's first of many writing's which is currently blessing the lives of God's people. November 2016 Pastor Nikki launched The Legacy ALC Heart Awareness Foundation, In Honor of her late husband this foundation was founded to educate families who have loved ones with a diagnosis of CHF, High Blood Pressure, and Diabetes. Annually the ministry will host a health education day to help save the lives of others. Harvest Springs Ministries is covered by Bishop I.V & Pastor Bridget Hilliard of New Light Christian Church, Houston Tx . As the Lord continues to elevate her from faith to faith and glory to glory she will continue strong in the faith walk of life. Pastor Nikki realizes that the enthusiasm and love for people has made her an inspiration to so many, and for this cause, she is determined to serve God and his people. Pastor Nikki continues to run with the vision that was founded July 2008 with the assistance of her current husband Pastor Kimball Boyd together they have 6 children and 2 grands.

AUVI CANADY is a successful business owner who started out at the age of eleven doing hair and found a love and passion for arts as it relates to becoming one of the greatest Make Up Artist at the age of 21. Auvi is a licensed master cosmetologist who also designs units for some of God's greatest gifts in the body of Christ. In 2016 Auvi launched Legacy ALC Hair Line , In honor of her late father who pushed her beyond her limits to create wealth for herself. Although the hair industry is of a wide stream, this hair line was designed for the everyday woman. Since the young tender age of ten Auvi has always had the passion to draw other's she was a part of the drama team growing up and she does this well with no effort. Growing up with two parents was rare in her circle of friends and this she didn't take for granted. Today she takes a greater approach and she moves forward in focusing on the call on her life which is to reach the millennia's. Fall 2018 Auvi will host her first of many youth explosion which will also include a segment with PK's.

To Contact the Authors, Go To:

Facebook: Nikki Canady-Boyd
Instagram: Pastor_Nikki
Twitter: PastorNikkiCB
Facebook: Auvi Canady-Jones

www.ingramcontent.com/pod-product-compliance
Lightning Source LLC
Chambersburg PA
CBHW052104070526
44584CB00017B/2328